PREPARATION *for* SUFFERING

JOHN FLAVEL

Preparation for Suffering

is a revised edition of

Preparations for Suffering, or
The Best Work in the Worst of Times

By John Flavel (1628-1691)
Published by W. Baynes and Son, 1820

This work is taken from
The Works of John Flavel, VOLUME VI
Banner of Truth, 1968, reprinted 1997

published by

▥ CORNER PILLAR PRESS
Forest, VA
© 2011 Jennifer Adams
All Rights Reserved

Printed in the United States of America

ISBN: 978-0-9844320-3-5

cornerpillarpress@gmail.com
www.cornerpillarpress.com

Front Cover: Charles T. Webber, 1891

This book is lovingly dedicated to

Mary Bethany Adams
Elisabeth Victoria Adams
Sarah Kate Adams
Anna Grace Adams

May the Lord grace you to
Manifest His beauty and display His worth
By imitating His Son in submitting
To the crosses He lovingly gives you for
His glory and your eternal joy.

Other Works from CORNER PILLAR PRESS:

*The Fountain of Life: A Display of Christ in His Essential
and Mediatorial Glory*, by John Flavel
*The Return of Prayers: Sowing Seeds of Prayer
and Waiting on God for a Harvest of Answers*,
by Thomas Goodwin
Importunity: Refusing to Give Up in Prayer,
by Christopher Love
*The God Who Answers Prayer:
The Work of the Father, Son, and Spirit in Prayer*,
by David Clarkson

"Completer to a Contender for the Faith" Series:
A Basket of Summer Fruit, by Susannah Spurgeon
In Love with Christ: The Narrative of Sarah Edwards,
by Sarah Edwards
Ann Judson: Missionary Wife, VOLUME I of
The Lives of the Three Mrs. Judsons, by Arabella Stuart,
Revised, edited, and expanded by Jennifer Adams
*Delighting in Her Heavenly Bridegroom:
The Memoirs of Harriet Newell, Teenage Missionary Wife*
Edited and annotated by Jennifer Adams
*Following Her Beloved: The Memoirs of Henrietta Shuck,
Missionary Wife and Mother*,
Compiled by Jeremiah Bell Jeter
Edited and expanded by Jennifer Adams
*With Cords of Love: The Memoirs of Elizabeth Dwight:
Missionary Wife and Mother*,
Compiled by Harrison Dwight
Edited and expanded by Jennifer Adams

CONTENTS

PREFACE

This edition of *Preparation for Suffering* is the original, unabridged edition with a few minor revisions to punctuation, grammar, and vocabulary. Every effort has been made to preserve the beauty of the "Old English" resonance while still making it comprehensible for today's reader.

Scripture references have been converted from Roman numerals to Arabic, chapter titles have been added, and archaic words have been defined in the footnotes. A detailed outline has been provided in the appendix to help the reader follow the flow of thought and identify main points.

Special thanks to Mary Bethany Adams for proofreading the text, and Courtney Joshua for proofreading the biographical sketch. May the Lord bless you, dear reader, through this work, and may He use it to prepare His church to glorify Him, in life and in death.

JOHN FLAVEL

 John Flavel was no stranger to suffering. He witnessed the imprisonment and death of his parents for their faith, was widowed three times, lost one infant son to death, was forcibly removed from the congregation he loved, lived under house arrest, and preached on the run in woods, caves, and in secret house meetings. He suffered from bodily weakness and the harsh conditions of living in the seventeenth century. He constantly put his life in danger to bring the gospel to the people of England. He poured himself out like a drink offering upon the sacrifice and service of their faith—and ours.[1] He considered Christ worthy, willing to share in the fellowship of His sufferings.

John was born in 1628 in Bromsgrove, Worcestershire, England.[2] He was the son of Richard Flavel, a nonconformist preacher who diligently taught his son the Scriptures. John spoke most tenderly of his father and the primary role he had in his conversion and spiritual growth. John attended Oxford University at any early age and excelled in his studies. After graduating, he became a minister's assistant to Mr. Walplate of Diptford.

In 1665, both his mother and father were arrested during a private prayer meeting and put in a plague-infested prison. Shortly thereafter, they died. Their faithfulness to "preach the Word in season and out"[3] and their willingness to lay down their lives for Christ lived on in their sons, both of whom became preachers of the gospel.

---

[1] See below his prayer for God's blessing upon his written works.
[2] Information for this biographical sketch is drawn primarily from *The Life of the Late Rev. Mr. John Flavel: Minister of Dartmouth*, The Works of John Flavel, Vol. 1, Banner of Truth, 1968.
[3] II Timothy 4:2

John married Jane Randal, a pious woman from a good family. However, after a short period of time, she died in child-birth. A year later John married Elizabeth Morris, a godly woman who was a completer to him in every sense of the term. At that time he took a pastorate at Dartmouth. The Lord graced his ministry with many conversions. One parishioner spoke of him saying, "In short, that person must have a very soft head, or a very hard heart, or both, who could sit under his ministry unaffected." He applied himself diligently to study, prayer, and meditation. He was said to have an excellent gift of prayer by which "he always brought with him a broken heart and moving affections. His tongue and spirit were touched with a live coal from the altar, and he was evidently assisted by the Holy Spirit of grace and supplication." His family members said that "he was always full and copious in prayer." He was an affectionate husband and father.

He ministered during the Uniformity Act in England, which meant that he lived under the constant threat of prison, banishment, or death for preaching the gospel. But he never missed a Lord's Day. Whether meeting in woods or in private homes, he continually risked his life to feed the sheep.

During this tenuous time, his wife Elizabeth, who was a kindred spirit in the Lord and an indispensable helpmate in the ministry, died. John felt her loss acutely and grieved deeply. In the course of time, he married a woman named Ann Downe, with whom he had a happy marriage of eleven years and two sons.

After Ann died, John married the daughter of George Jeffries, a minister at King's-Bridge. For a brief time, John was under house arrest. Many of his flock came late at night or before dawn to hear him preach and worship together in prayer, song, and holy discourse.

In 1687, he preached a sermon from Revelation 3:20, "Behold I stand at the door and knock," which was greatly used of the Lord for the conversion of many. He preached twice every Lord's Day, lectured every Wednesday, and preached every Thursday before the Lord's Supper. "He allowed himself very little recreation, accounting time a precious jewel that ought to be improved at any rate. . . . He preached what he felt, what he handled, what he had seen and tasted of the Word of life, and his people felt it. . . . He was a mighty wrestler with God in secret prayer, and particularly begged of Him to crown his sermons, printed books, and private discourses with the conversion of sinners, a work which his heart was much set upon." May the Lord continue to answer those prayers through the reprinting of this book—for His glory and the advancement of His great Name.

FOREWORD

Humiliation for our own sins and the due preparation to take up our own cross and follow Christ in a suffering path is the only mark and aim of this tract.

The expectation of and preparation for suffering abates much of its dread and terror by accustoming our thoughts beforehand to them, that we may find them not so grievous, shocking, and intolerable when they come.

Reader, the cup of suffering is a very bitter cup, and it is needful that we provide something to sweeten it so that we may be able to receive it with thanksgiving. What those sweetening ingredients are, and how to prepare them, you will have some direction and help in the following discourse.

It is a blessed and excellent thing for the people of God to be prepared and ready for the hardest services and worst of suffering to which the Lord may call them. Beloved, suffering is one of the choicest discoveries of your love to your master Christ—yea, it is such a testimony of love to him as angels are not capable of. They show their love by their readiness to do his will in the execution of which they fly as with wings (Ezekiel 1:24), but you only have the happiness of testifying your love for him by your readiness to suffer for him. Is not this excellent? The shoe of preparation to follow him through thorns and briers, and over rocks and mountains of difficulties and troubles, *loves him indeed.*

PREPARATION

FOR

SUFFERING:

OR

THE BEST WORK IN THE WORST OF TIMES

Wherein the Necessity, Excellency, and Means of our readiness for Suffering are evinced and prescribed; our Call to suffering cleared, and the great unreadiness of many professors bewailed.

THE EPISTLE TO THE READER

IT was the observation of the learned Gerson (when the world was not as old as it is now) that *mundus senescens patitur phantasias*, that is, the aged world, liked aged persons, dotes and grows whimsical in its old age. The truth of this observation is confirmed by nothing more than the fond and groundless dreams of tranquility and continuing prosperity with which the multitude please themselves, even whilst the sins of the times are so great and the signs of the times so sad and lowering as they are.

It is not the design of this book to scare and affright any man with imaginary dangers, much less to sow jealousies and foster discontent. It is a just matter of lamentation that all the tokens of God's anger produce with many of us no better fruit than bold censures and loud clamors instead of humiliation for our own sins and the due preparation to take up our own cross

15

and follow Christ in a suffering path, which is the only mark and aim of this tract.

We read the histories of the primitive Christians who suffered for their faith in Christ but not with a spirit prepared to follow them. Some censure them as too prodigal of their blood and others commend their courage and constancy, but where are they that sincerely resolve and prepare to be followers of them "who through faith and patience inherit the promises" (Heb. 6:12)? Or where are they who take them for an "example of suffering, affliction, and of patience" (Jam. 5:10)?

It is as much our interest as it is our duty to be seasonably awakened out of our pleasant but most dangerous drowsiness. Troubles will be so much the more sinking and intolerable by how much the more they steal upon us by way of surprise. For as expectation deflowers any temporal comfort by sucking out much of the sweetness thereof beforehand, and so we find the less in it when we come to the actual enjoyment, so the expectation of evil abates much of the dread and terror by accustoming our thoughts beforehand to them and making preparation for them that we find them not so grievous, shocking, and intolerable when they are come indeed.

This was exemplified to us very lively by Mr. Bradford, the martyr, when the keeper's wife came running into his chamber saying, "O Mr. Bradford, I bring you heavy tidings! For tomorrow you must be burned! Your chain is now being bought, and presently you must go to Newgate." Mr. Bradford took off his hat and looking up to heaven said, "O Lord, I thank thee for it. I have looked for this a long time. It comes not suddenly to me. The Lord make me worthy of it." See in this example the singular advantage of a prepared and ready soul.

Reader, the cup of suffering is a very bitter cup, and it is but needful that we provide something to sweeten it so that we may be able to receive it with thanksgiving. What those sweetening ingredients are, and how to prepare them, you will have some direction and help in the following discourse, which hath once already been presented to the public view, and that it may at this time also (wherein nothing can be more seasonable) become further useful and assisting to the people of God in their present duties, is the hearty desire of...

Thine and the Church's Servant in Christ,
JOHN FLAVEL

CHAPTER I

Prepare to Suffer

Then Paul answered, "What mean ye to weep and to break my heart? For I am ready not to be bound only, but also to die at Jerusalem for the name of the Lord Jesus" (Acts 21:13).

The Text Explained and the Doctrine Propounded

THE Divine providence is not more singularly discovered in governing the motions of the clouds than it is in disposing and ordering the spirits and motions of the ministers of the gospel, who, in a mystical sense, are fruitful clouds to dispense the showers of gospel blessings to the world. The motion of the clouds is not spontaneous, but they move as they are moved by the winds. Neither can gospel ministers choose their own stations and govern their own motions but must go when and where the Spirit and providence of God directs and guides them, as will evidently appear in that dangerous voyage to Jerusalem in which the apostle was at this time engaged. "And now, behold, I go bound in the Spirit to Jerusalem" (Acts 20:22). This is alluding to the watery vapors which are bound up in the clouds and conveyed according to the motions of the wind. This journey was full of danger. Paul foresaw his business was not only to plant the gospel at Jerusalem with his doctrine but to water it with his blood, yet so effectually was his will determined by the will of God that he cheerfully complied with his duty therein, whatsoever difficulties and dangers did attend it.

And indeed, it was his great advantage that the will of God was so plainly and convincingly revealed to him touching this matter. For no sooner did he employ himself to obey this call of God but he was presently assaulted by many strong temptations to decline it.

The first rub he met with in his way was from the disciples of Tyre, who pretending to speak by the Spirit, said unto Paul that he should not go up to Jerusalem (Acts 21:4). The Lord by this tested the spirit of his apostle much, as he did with the young prophet coming from Judea to Bethel (1 Kings 13:18).

His next discouragement was at Caesarea, where Agabus (whom Dorotheus affirms to be one of the seventy-two disciples, and who had before prophesied of the famine in the reign of Claudius which accordingly came to pass) took Paul's girdle, and binding his own hands and feet with it said, "Thus said the Holy Ghost, 'So shall the Jews at Jerusalem bind the man that owns this girdle, and shall deliver him into the hands of the Gentiles'" (Acts 21:11). And surely he was not ignorant what he must expect whenever he should fall into their hands; yet neither could this affright him from his duty.

But then, last of all, he met with the sorest trial from his dearest friends, who fell upon him with passionate entreaties and many tears beseeching him to decline that journey. O they could not give up such a minister as Paul! This melted him down and almost broke his heart, which was easier to do than to turn him out of the path of obedience. Where, by the way, we may note two things.

First, that divine precept, not providence, is to rule our way of duty. Secondly, no hindrances or discouragements whatsoever will justify our neglect of a known duty.

All these rubs he passed over, and all these discouragements he overcame with this heroic and truly Christian resolution in the text, "What mean ye to weep, and to break my heart? For I am ready not to be bound only, but also to die at Jerusalem for the name of the Lord Jesus" (Acts 21:13).

In this text we have:
1. A loving and gentle rebuke
2. A quieting and calming argument

First, He lovingly and gently rebukes their fond and inordinate sorrow for his departure in these words, "*What mean ye to weep, and to break my heart?*" It is as if he should say, "Why these passionate entreaties and tempting tears? To what purpose is all this ado? They are but so many snares of Satan to turn my heart out of the way of obedience. You do as much as in you lies to break my heart; let there be no more of this I beseech you."

Secondly, He labors to charm their unruly passions with a very quieting and calming argument, "*For I am ready*" *parate habeo.* I am prepared and fitted for the greatest suffering which shall befall me in the pursuit of my duty; be it a prison, or be it death, I am ready for either. Liberty is dear, and life dearer still, but Christ is dearer than either.

But what was there in all this to satisfy them whose trouble it was to see him so forward? Let the words be considered, and we shall find divers things in them to satisfy and quiet their hearts and make them willing to give him up.

First, "I am ready." That is, God hath fitted and prepared my heart for the greatest suffering. This is the work of God. Flesh and blood would never be brought to this were not all its interests and inclinations subdued and over-ruled by the Spirit of God. What you are doing is working against the design of God who hath fitted and prepared my heart for this service.

21

Secondly, "I am ready." That is, my will and resolution stand in a full bent and my heart is fixed. You cannot, therefore, do me a greater injury than to discompose and disorder my heart again by casting such temptations as these in my way to cause the flesh to rebel and the enemy that is within to renew his opposition.

Thirdly, "I am ready." That is, my heart is so fixed to follow the call of God, whatever shall befall me, that all your tears and entreaties to the contrary are but cast away. They cannot alter my fixed purpose. You had as good be quiet and cheerfully resign me to the will of God.

Thus you see the equipage and preparation of Paul's spirit to receive both bonds and death for Christ at Jerusalem. This made him victorious over the temptations of friends and the malice and cruelty of his enemies. By this readiness and preparation of his mind, he was carried through all and enabled to finish his course with joy. From hence the observation is:

Doctrine: *That it is a blessed and excellent thing for the people of God to be prepared and ready for the hardest services and worst of suffering to which the Lord may call them.*

This is that which every gracious heart is reaching after, praying for, and striving to obtain. But ah! How few will attain it! Certainly there are not many among the multitudes of the professors of this generation that can say as Paul here did, "I am ready to be bound, or to die for Christ."

22

CHAPTER II

Why God Calls His People to Suffer

Acts 21:13 shows that although God takes no delight in afflicting his people, he sometimes exposes them to great and grievous suffering, with a brief account of why and how he calls them thereunto.

THE mercies and compassions of God over his people are exceedingly great and tender. "Like as a father pities his children, so the Lord pities them that fear him" (Psalm 103:13). He does not delight in afflicting and grieving them. "He doth not afflict willingly nor grieve the children of men" (Lam. 3:33). The scripture intimates to us a seeming conflict betwixt the justice and mercy of God when he is about to deliver up his people into their enemies' hands. "How shall I give thee up, Ephraim? How shall I deliver thee, Israel? How shall I make thee as Admah? How shall I set thee as Zeboim? Mine heart is turned within me, my repentings are kindled together" (Hosea 11:8-9). This shows us with what reluctance and great unwillingness the Lord goes about such a work as this. The work of judgment is his *strange work*. It pleases him better to execute the milder attribute of mercy towards his children. Hence, we find that when he is preparing to execute his judgments, he delays the execution as long as the honor of his name and safety of his people will permit (Jer. 44:23). He bears till he can bear no longer. He often turns away his wrath from them (Psalm 78:38-39). He tries them by lesser judgments and gentler corrections to prevent greater judgments (Amos 4:6). When his people are humbled under the threatenings of his wrath, his heart is melted into

23

compassion to them (Jer. 31:17-20). Whenever his mercy prevails against judgment, it is with joy and triumph (Jam. 2:13). *Mercy rejoices against judgment.*

He feels his own tender compassions yearning over them. He foresees and is in no way willing to gratify the insulting pride of his and their enemies. "I said I would scatter them into corners, I would make the remembrance of them to cease from among men were it not that I feared the wrath of the enemy, lest their adversaries should behave themselves strangely" (Deut. 32:26-27).

Yet all this, notwithstanding, it often falls out by the provocations of his sons and daughters that the Lord gives them up into the hands of their enemies for the correction of their evils and the manifestation of his own glory. Seneca, though a heathen, could say that God loves his people with a masculine love not with a womanly indulgence and tenderness. If need require, they shall be in heaviness through manifold temptations (1 Pet. 1:6). He had rather their hearts should be heavy under adversity than vain and careless under prosperity. The choicest spirits have been exercised with the sharpest sufferings, and those that now shine as stars in heaven have been trod under foot as dung on the earth. "Unto this present hour we both hunger and thirst, and are naked, and buffeted, and have no certain dwelling-place, and labor, working with our hands; being reviled we bless, being persecuted we suffer it, being defamed we entreat; we are made as the filth of the world, and the off-scouring of all things unto this day" (I Cor. 4:11-12). The eleventh chapter to the Hebrews is a compendium of the various and grievous sufferings of the primitive saints. "They were tortured, they were sawn asunder, were tempted, were slain with the sword, they wandered about in sheep-skins and goat-skins, being afflicted, destitute, tormented, of whom the world was not worthy. They wandered in deserts, and in mountains, in dens, and in caves of the earth." And since the earth hath dried up those rivers of precious blood whereof the sacred records make mention, what seas of Christians' blood have since those days been shed by bloody persecutors? Histories inform us that in the ten primitive persecutions, so many of the saints and martyrs of Jesus Christ have been slain that it adds up to five thousand a day to every day in the whole year. Those bloody emperors sported themselves with the death of God's dear saints. Many precious Christians were burnt by night at Rome to serve as torches to light their enemies in the passage through the streets. Eight hundred thousand martyrs are mentioned within the space of thirty years since the Jesuits arose out of the bottomless pit.

To what grievous sufferings did the Lord give up those precious servants of Christ, namely the Waldenses and Albigenses, who received the light of reformation about the year 1260 when the fogs of anti-Christian darkness overspread the earth! They were a people sound in judgment, as appears by their letters, catechisms, and confessions which are extant. They were a people of a simple, plain, and inoffensive behavior. Yet, with what fury and rage did that impious pope Pius persecute them to destruction! Driving them into the woods and mountains, except the aged and children that could not flee, who were murdered in the way. Some famished in the caves and clefts of the rocks; others endured the rack for eight hours together; some were beaten with iron rods, while others were thrown from the tops of high towers and dashed to pieces.

What bloody shambles and slaughter-houses have France, Ireland, and England been made by popish cruelty! More might be related out of each story than a tender-hearted reader is able to bear. But what God hath done, he may do again. We are not better than our fathers. Dismal clouds of indignation are gathering over our heads, charged with double destruction. Should the Lord please to make them break upon us, we cannot imagine the rage of Satan to be abated now that his kingdom hastens to its period (Rev. 12:12), nor have his instruments grown less cruel and skillful to destroy. The land indeed hath enjoyed a long rest, and this generation is acquainted with little more of martyrdom than what the histories of former times inform us of. Yet, let no man befool himself with a groundless expectation of continuing tranquility. Augustine thinks that the bloody sweat which over-ran the body of Christ in the garden signified the sharp and grievous sufferings which in his mystical body he should afterward endure. Indeed, it is a truth that these are also called the remains of Christ's sufferings (Col. 1:24). His *personal sufferings* were indeed completed at his resurrection. That cup was full to the brim, to which no drop of sufferings can be added. But his sufferings in his mystical body are not yet full. By his personal sufferings, he fully satisfied the wrath of God, but the sufferings of his people have not yet satisfied the wrath of men. Though millions of precious saints have shed their blood for Christ, whose souls are now crying under the altar, "*How long, Lord! How long!*" yet there are many more coming on behind in the same path of persecution. Much Christian blood must yet be shed before the mystery of God be finished. Notwithstanding this lucid interval, the clouds seem to be returning again after the rain. Thus, you see to what grievous sufferings the merciful God hath sometimes called his dearest people.

Now God may be said to call forth his people to suffer when he hedges them in by providence so that there is no way to escape suffering but by sin. Whatsoever providence labors with such a dilemma as this is a plain signification of God's will to us in that case. We may not now expect extraordinary calls to suffering work, as some of the saints had of old (Gen. 22:2; Acts 9:16), but when our way is so shut up by providence that we cannot avoid suffering but by stepping over the hedge of the command, God will have us look upon that exigence as his call to suffer. And if the reasons be demanded why the Lord, who is inclined to mercy, doth often hedge in his own people by his providence in a suffering path, let us know that in so doing he doth both:

1. Illustrate his own glory
2. Promote his people's happiness

First, Hereby the most wise God doth illustrate the glory of his own name, clearing up the righteousness of his ways by the sufferings of his own people. By this the world shall see that however much he loves them, he will not indulge or patronize their sins. If they will be so disingenuous to abuse his favors, he will be so just as to make them suffer for their sins—and by those very sufferings he will provide for his own glory, which was by them clouded in the eyes of the world. He hates not sin a jot the less because it is found in his own people (Amos 3:2). And though, for the magnifying of his mercy, he will pardon their sins, yet for the clearing of his righteousness, he will take vengeance upon their inventions (Psalm 99:8).

Moreover, by exposing his people to such grievous sufferings, he gives a fit opportunity to manifest the glory of his power in their support and of his wisdom in the marvelous ways of their escape and deliverance. It is one of the greatest wonders in the world how the church subsists under such fierce and frequent assaults as are made upon it by enemies. "I will turn aside (said Moses) and see this great sight, why the bush is not consumed" (Ex. 3:3). That flaming bush was a lively emblem of the oppressed church in Egypt. The crackling flames noted the heat of their persecution. The remaining of the bush unconsumed in the flames signified the wonderful power of God in their preservation. No people are so privileged, so protected, and so delivered as the people of God. Much less opposition than hath been made against the church has overturned and utterly destroyed the mighty monarchies of the world.

> *Sic Medus ademit*
> *Assyrio, Medoque tulit moderamina Perses,*
> *Subject Persen Macedo, cessurus et ipse*
> *Romanis*[4]

> Assyria's empire thus the Mede did shake,
> The Persian next, the pride of Media brake;
> Then Persia sunk by Macedonia prest,
> That, in its turn, fell by Rome at Last.

And no less admirable is the wisdom of God in frustrating and defeating the most deep and desperate designs of hell against his poor people. Now, you may see the most wise God going beyond a malicious and subtle devil by overturning in a moment the deep laid designs and contrivances of many years, and that at the very birth and point of execution (Esther 6:1), by snaring the wicked in the works of their own hands, making their own tongues to fall upon them and working out such marvellous salvations with his own hand as fills them with astonishment and wonder. "When the Lord turned back the captivity of Zion, we were like them that dreamed" (Psalm 126:7).

---

[4] Claudian, lib. 3. in laudes Stillicones.

Secondly, As God provides for his own glory by the sufferings and troubles of his people, so he advances their happiness and greatly promotes their interest thereby. For,

(1.) These troubles are ordered as occasions and means to mortify the corruptions that are in their hearts. There are rank weeds springing up in the best soil which need such winter weather to rot them. And certainly, if we reckon humility, heavenly mindedness, contempt of the world, and longing desires after heaven to be the real interest and advantage of the church, then it is evident that nothing so much promotes their interest as a suffering condition doth. Adversity kills those corruptions which prosperity bred.

(2.) By these trials, the sincerity of their faith is cleared to the joy and satisfaction of their own hearts. Many a doubt and fear which had long entangled and perplexed them is removed and answered. When adversity hath given them proof and trial of their own hearts, one sharp trial wherein God helps us to be faithful will do more to satisfy our fears and resolve our doubts than all the sermons we ever heard in our lives could do.

(3.) These sufferings and trials of the church are ordained to free it of hypocrites, which were its reproach as well as burden (Amos 9:9-10). Affliction is a furnace to separate the dross from the more pure and noble gold. Multitudes of hypocrites, like flies in a hot summer, are generated by the church's prosperity—but winter weather kills them. Many gaudy professors grow within the enclosure of the church like beautiful flowers in the field. They stand there during its peace and prosperity in the pride and bravery of their gifts and professions, but the wind passes over them and they are gone, and their places shall know them no more (Psalm 103:16). Thunder and lightning are very terrible weather but exceeding useful to purify and cleanse the air.

29

Fourthly, The church's sufferings are ordered and sanctified to endear them to each other. Times of common suffering are times of reconciliation and greater endearments among the people of God. Never more endeared than when most persecuted; never more united than when most scattered. "Then they that feared the Lord spoke often one to another" (Mal. 3:16). Certainly there is something in our fellowship in the same suffering that is endearing and engaging; but there is much more in the discoveries that persecution makes of the sincerity of our hearts, which, it may be, was before entertained with jealousy. Yet more than all this there is the reproofs of the rod, whereby they are humbled for their pride, wantonness, and bitterness of their spirits to each other, and made to cry in the sense of these transgressions, "Remember not against us our former iniquities" (Psalm 79:8).

Lastly, By these troubles and distresses, they are awakened to their duties and taught to pray more frequently, spiritually, and fervently. Ah! What drowsiness and formality is apt to creep in upon the best hearts in the time of prosperity; but when the storm rises and the sea grows turbulent and raging, now they cry as the disciples to Christ, "*Lord, save us, we perish!*" They say music is sweetest upon the waters. I am sure the sweetest melody of prayer is upon the deep waters of affliction. For these among many other righteous, wise, and holy ends the Lord permits and orders the persecutions and distresses of his people.

CHAPTER III

Forewarnings of Suffering

Acts 21:13 shows that it is usual with God to premonish his people of approaching trials and sufferings with some account of the manner how and the reason why he so forewarns them.

AS Paul had many clear premonitions and forewarnings of the sufferings that should befall him at Jerusalem so that he might not be surprised by them when they came, so it is usual with God (though not in such an immediate and extraordinary manner) to admonish the world, and especially his own people, of great trials and sufferings beforehand. "Surely the Lord will do nothing but he reveals his secrets unto his servants the prophets" (Amos 3:7).

Thus, when he was about to bring the flood upon the world, he gave one hundred and twenty years warning of it before it came (Gen. 6:3). When he was to destroy Sodom, he said, "Shall I hide from Abraham the thing that I do?" (Gen. 18:17) And the like discovery he made about the same judgment to Lot (Gen. 19:12-14). So when the captivity of the Jews was nigh at hand, the people had many forewarnings of it. God forewarned them both ministerially and providentially. He warned them by the prophets, "Hear the word of my mouth, and give them warning from me" (Ezek. 3:17). And when the time drew nigh to execute the judgment determined upon Jerusalem and the temple, how plainly did Christ foretell them of it? "Thine enemies shall cast a trench about thee, and compass thee round, and keep thee in on every side, and shall lay thee even with the ground, and thy children with thee" (Luke 19:43-44).

And when the storm was just ready to fall, their own historian tells us that a voice was heard in the temple saying, "Migremus hinc" that is, "*Let us go hence.*"[5] Tacitus also made reference to this voice in his annals, affirming it to be more than a human voice telling them that God was departing, and it was said to be accompanied with a rushing noise as of persons going out.[6] These were extraordinary warnings. The like signs have been given to divers other nations by dreadful eclipses of the heavenly bodies, portentous comets, earthquakes, and other signs of judgment.

Now, though we have no ground to expect such extraordinary warnings, yet we have the most apparent and certain signs of approaching calamities, after which, if they surprise us, the fault must lie in our own inexcusable negligence. For we have a standing rule to govern ourselves in this matter, and that is, "When the same sins are found in one nation which have brought down the wrath of God upon another nation, it is an evident sign of judgment at the door, for God is unchangeable, just, and holy. He will not favor that in one people which he hath punished in another, nor bless that in one age which he hath punished in another, nor bless that in one age which he hath cursed in another." Upon this very ground it was that the apostle warned the Corinthians by the example of the Israelites whose sins had ruined them in the wilderness, "Now these things were our examples to the intent we should not lust after evil things as they also lusted" (I Cor. 10:6). As if he should say, "Look upon those dead bodies which are, as it were, cast up upon the scripture-shore for a

---

[5] Josephus de bello Jud. lib. 7. cap. 2.
[6] Audita major humana vox excedere Deos, simul ingens motus excedentium. Tacitus, lib. 21.

warning to you. Follow not the same course, lest you meet in the same curse. If you tread the same paths, expect the same punishment. God is as righteous now as he was then. He hates sin and will punish it in you as much as he did in them.

Let us, therefore, consider what those provocations were that hastened the wrath of God upon his own Israel, a people that were nigh and dear unto him—a people upon whom he spent as much of the riches of his patience as upon any people in the world—so that we may reckon whereabout we are at this day and what it is like to be the lot of this sinful and provoking generation. We shall find by the consent of all the prophets that these sins were the immediate forerunners and proper causes of their overthrow.

First, The great corruption of God's worship among them kindled his wrath and hastened their ruin. "They were defiled with their own works and went a whoring with their own inventions; therefore was the wrath of God kindled against his people insomuch that he abhorred his own inheritance, and he gave them into the hand of the heathen, and they that hated them that ruled over them; their enemies also oppressed them, and they were brought into subjection under their hand" (Psalm 106:39-42). They that will not bear the golden yoke of Christ shall be galled[7] with the iron yoke of men. Nothing more provokes the anger of God than the adulterating of his worship. A man will bear a thousand infirmities in the wife of his bosom, but unfaithfulness in the marriage-covenant breaks his heart. After the manner of men, so abused and grieved, the Lord expressed himself, "I am broken with their whorish hearts which have departed from me and with their eyes that go a whoring after their idols" (Ezek. 6:9). Men cannot invent

---

[7] vexed, chafed by

a surer and speedier way to their own ruin than to bring their own inventions into God's worship.

Secondly, Incorrigible obstinacy and impenitency under gentler strokes and lesser judgments make way for utter ruin and desolation (Amos 4:6-12). Scarcity, mildews, pestilence, and sword had been tried upon them but without effect—for the remnant that escaped those judgments (although plucked as so many brands out of the fire in which their fellow sinners perished) were not reformed by those gentler and moderated judgments.

Thirdly, Spiritual dullness and senselessness of God's hand and the tokens of his anger were provoking causes and forerunners to their national desolation. They neither saw the hand of God when it was lifted up nor humbled themselves under it when it was laid on. The hand of God is then said to be lifted up when the providences of God prepare and posture themselves for our affliction. When the clouds of judgment gather over our heads and grow blacker and blacker as theirs did upon them, but they took no notice of it, the hand of judgment is near. "Lord, when thy hand is lifted up they will not see" (Is. 26:11). It is the height of spiritual blindness to remain senseless when the hand of God is upon us. "Who gave Jacob for a spoil and Israel to the robbers? Did not the Lord, he against whom we have sinned? For they would not walk in his ways, neither were they obedient to his law. Therefore, he hath poured upon them the fury of his anger and the strength of battle; and it hath set them on fire round about, yet they knew not; and it burned them, yet they laid it not to heart" (Is. 42:24-25).

O prodigious drunkenness! It was not some small drops of God's anger but the fury of his wrath. It was not some light skirmish of his judgments with them but the strength of battle. It was not some particular stroke upon a single person or family, but it set him on fire round about, a general conflagration—yet all this would not awaken them.

Fourthly, The persecution of God's faithful ministers and people were another sin that procured and a sign that foretold the destruction of their nation. "And the Lord God of their fathers sent to them by his messengers, rising up betimes and sending because he had compassion on his people, and on his dwelling-place; but they mocked the messengers of God and despised his words and misused his prophets until the wrath of the Lord arose against his people, till there was no remedy" (II Chron. 36:15-16). There were also a number of upright souls among them who desired to worship God according to his own prescription, but a snare was laid for them in Mizpah and a net spread for them upon Tabor (Hos. 5:1) which hastened judgment towards Israel. Mizpah and Tabor were places lying in the way between Samaria and Jerusalem where the true worship of God was. In those places, spies were set by the priests to observe and inform against those who sought the Lord so that it became very hazardous to attend the pure and incorrupt worship of God which quickly hastened on the ruin of the nation.

Fifthly, The removal of godly and useful men by death in more than ordinary haste was to them a sign of desolation at hand. "The righteous perishes, and no man lays it to heart, and merciful men are taken away, none considering that the righteous is taken away from the evil to come" (Is. 57:1). In this case, God acts towards his people as the husbandman in a catching harvest doth by his corn—he hurries it with a shuffling haste into the barn when he sees a storm coming. Or, he acts as a careful father with his sons that are abroad at school, who sends his horses to fetch them speedily when he hears the plague is begun in the place. Upon this ground the prophet Micah bewails himself. "Woe is me, for I am as when they have gathered the summer-fruits, as the grape gleanings of the vintage, there is no cluster to eat; my soul desired the first-ripe fruit" (Mic. 7:1). Alas! Alas! What miserable days are at hand! What miseries must I expect to see! The pleasant clusters, i.e., the societies of the saints, are gathered away by the hand of death. There are but few that remain—here and there is a single saint, like grapes after the vintage is done, two or three upon the utmost branches.

Sixthly, The general decay of the life and power of godliness among them that were left foreboded destruction at the door. This is both a provoking sin and a fore-running sign of national calamity. Hosea 4:18, "their drink is sour," serves as a metaphor, lively expressing the deadness and formality of the people in the worship of God, likening it to sour or dead drink which hath lost its spirit and become flat. Such were their religious duties—there was no spiritual life, affection, or savor in them. They heard as if they heard not and prayed as if they prayed not. The ordinances of God were to them as the ordinances of men of which the apostle said that they perish in the using.

Seventhly, To conclude, mutual animosities, jars, and divisions were to them manifest symptoms of national calamities and desolations, for then Ephraim envied Judah and Judah vexed Ephraim. "The days of visitation are come, the days of recompense are come, Israel shall know it. The prophet is a fool, the spiritual man is mad, for the multitude of thine iniquities, and the great hatred" (Is. 11:13; Hos. 9:7).

When such symptoms of God's indignation do appear upon any people, the Lord, by them, as by so many glaring meteors and blazing comets, forewarns the world that his judgments are near, even at the door. These signs all men ought to observe and behold with trembling. If you ask, "Why doth

36

God usually give such warnings of his indignation before it comes?"

The reasons are:
1. To prevent the execution
2. To make them more tolerable
3. To leave the incorrigible inexcusable

First, Warning is given with design to prevent the execution of judgments. "Therefore thus will I do unto thee, O Israel; and because I will do this unto thee, prepare to meet thy God, O Israel" (Amos 4:12). Prepare thyself to meet me in the way of my judgments by humiliation and intercession to prevent the execution. And what else was the design of God in sending Jonah to the great city Ninevah but to excite them to repentance for the prevention of their ruin. This Jonah knew to be the Lord's meaning, how positive whatsoever the words of his commission were. Therefore, he declined the message to secure his credit, knowing that if upon warning they repented, the gracious nature of God would soon melt into compassion over them, and free grace would make Jonah appear as a liar, for so we must expound his words, "Was not this my saying when I was yet in my country? Therefore, I fled before unto Tarshish, for I knew that thou art a gracious God, and merciful, slow to anger, and of great kindness, and repentest thee of the evil" (Jonah 4:2). Yea, Lord, I knew beforehand it would come to this; thou sendest me positively to denounce thy judgments to Ninevah, in the meantime desiring nothing more than that the execution of them might be prevented by their repentance. And thus thy mercy hath exposed my reputation in saving them from destruction.

Secondly, God forewarns his people of judgments to make them more tolerable when they come. Expected evils are not as heavy as those that come by surprise. For look, as the expectation of a mercy makes it less sweet, our thoughts having anticipated and sucked out much of the sweetness beforehand, so the expectation of judgments before they befall us makes them less bitter and burdensome than they otherwise would be since the soul has accustomed itself to them by frequent thoughts and prepared itself to entertain them, as Paul did in my text. To prevent the disciples surprise and offense at those days of persecution that were coming upon them, Christ foretold them and gave them fair warning beforehand (John 16:4).

Thirdly, He forewarns his people of approaching dangers to leave the incorrigible wholly inexcusable, that those who have no sense of sin, nor care to prevent ruin, might have no cloak for their folly when judgments overtake them. "What wilt thou say when he shall punish thee?" (Jer. 13:21-22). As if he should say, "What plea or apology is left thee after so many fair warnings and timely premonitions? Thou canst not say that I have surprised thee or that thou was ruined before thou was warned. Thy destruction, therefore, is of thyself."

CHAPTER IV

The Necessity of a Prepared Heart

Acts 21:23 demonstrates the excellency of a prepared heart for the worst of sufferings and what a blessed thing it is to be ready to be bound or to die for Christ, as Paul here was.

I AM ready. O blessed frame of spirit! How hard but how happy is it to get a heart so tempered! Every Christian can say that I would be ready, and Lord make me ready for suffering, but few can say, I *am* ready, my heart is prepared and fitted for such a work. Yet this example shows us it is attainable. What a blessed thing it is to attain it the following particulars will abundantly convince us.

First, Readiness for suffering will bring the heart of a Christian to a holy rest and tranquility in a suffering hour and prevent that anxiety, perturbation, and distraction of mind which puts the sinking weight into afflictions. The more cares, fears, and troubles we have before our suffering comes, the more calm, quiet, and composed we are likely to be when our suffering comes. It is admirable to consider with what peace and patience Job entertained his troubles, which, considering the kinds, degrees, and manner in which they befell him, one would think they should at least have startled and amazed him and put his soul (as gracious and mortified as it was) into great disorder and confusion, but you find the contrary. Never did the patience of a man triumph at that rate over adversity. He worshiped God, owned his hand, and resigned himself up to his pleasure (Job 1:20-21). And whence was this? Surely had his troubles come by way of surprise, he could never have carried it at that rate; but in the days of his peace and

39

prosperity, he had prepared for such a day as this. "I was not in safety, neither had I rest, yet trouble came. The thing that I feared (said he) is come upon me" (Job 3:25-26). He laid it to heart before it came, and therefore it neither distracted nor broke his heart when it did come. In like manner, the prophet Habakkuk stood upon his watch-tower and made his observations by the word upon the probable events of providence, whereby he got a clear foresight of those troublesome days that were at hand, which though it made him tremble in himself, yet it gave him rest in the day of evil (Hab. 3:16-18). There is a twofold rest in the day of evil.

1. A rest of deliverance
2. A rest of contentment

It is a singular mercy to find rest in a man's own spirit—to enjoy inward peace and tranquility of mind when there is no rest without. And the way to obtain this is to foresee, count upon, and make due preparation for troublesome times beforehand. Evils that come by way of surprise are not only shocking but very frequently destructive evils. It is a sad aggravation to feel a misery before we fear it. Those calamities that find men secure do usually leave them desperate. The enemy that comes upon our backs hath a great advantage to ruin us, yet this is the common case of the world. "For man knoweth not his time, but as the fishes are taken in an evil net, and as the birds that are caught in the snare, so are the sons of men snared in an evil time when it falleth on them suddenly" (Eccl. 9:12). Thus perished the old world. There was but one Noah provided for the flood, and he only, with his family, was preserved in it. All the rest were eating, drinking, marrying, and giving in marriage until the flood came and swept them all away (Matt. 24:38). Men will not use their

closure with Christ upon suffering and self-denying terms is by himself fully set forth in that excellent parable (Lk. 14:25-30). There was a great multitude that followed him at that time. Christ began to grow in request among them. They flocked from all parts to see and hear him, but he foresaw that if once a sharp trial should befall them, it would quickly thin and diminish that great multitude and reduce them, like Gideon's host, into a little handful. Therefore, he resolves to deal candidly and plainly with them. He propounds his terms and sets down his conditions to which every one of them must subscribe that will follow him. The sum of which is, "Let him deny himself, take up his cross, and follow me." And to evince the rationality of these terms, he argues from the most common and obvious practices of men in their civil affairs. No man that exercises reason will begin to build a house and lay a large foundation when he is not provided with a stock to carry up the walls and complete the work. No man in his wits would engage with a handful of men against a great and armed multitude. Possibly they may intend to face, but no man would think they intend to fight the enemy on such a disadvantage. Just so stands the case in our profession of Christ. If we really intend to go through with the business of religion, we must sit down and compute the cost of Christianity, think upon the worst as well as the best, reckon upon reproaches, prisons, and death for his sake as well as consider the easier and more pleasant parts of active obedience. Having so done, if then we can be content to run all hazards and forego all the rest upon his account and accordingly manage ourselves in a day of suffering, then we deal with Christ and clear ourselves from the danger of hypocrisy. It is for want of this that so many professors of the faith faint and fall away in times of temptation, furnishing the devil with so many triumphs over religion. It was for want of depth of earth (i.e. a deep

42

consideration and well-rooted resolution at first) that the stony-ground hypocrite so quickly withered away when the sun of persecution began to shine fervently upon him (Mt. 13:5-6). And doubtless it is to prevent this fatal issue of our profession that God makes such deep wounds by conviction upon his people's hearts at first. It is for our establishment in future trials and suffering that he so distresses and humbles them and makes sin so bitter and burdensome to them, well knowing that all this is no more than needed to prevent their returning again to sin in the times of temptation.

O professor of the faith! If thou be one that art come to Christ in this way and hast thus deliberately closed with him; if thou hast as well bethought thyself of bearing his cross as of wearing his crown, then thou hast a fair evidence of the uprightness of thy heart, of which the world cannot provide a sweeter comfort.

Thirdly, The advantage of preparation for suffering lies in this, that it prevents and cuts off the scandal and offense of the cross with respect both to ourselves and others.

(1.) It prevents our own offense at suffering. By Christ's own testimony the soul is blessed that is not offended in him (Matt. 11:6). Among the multitudes of professors of religion, few are found that are not offended when they are actually called to suffer for Christ. They expected much peace, honor, and prosperity in the ways of religion, but finding their expectations frustrated and their carnal interest rather exposed than secured by their profession of Christ, they go back like those in John 6:66 and walk no more with him. And it is very remarkable that Christ dates the offense that men shall take at him from the first appearance of suffering. "All these are the beginnings of sorrows, and then shall many be offended" (Mt. 24:8-9). Sorrows and apostasies commence together.

But reader, if thou be one that makes it thy business to foresee and prepare for an evil day, thou wilt have as good thoughts of Christ and his ways at the lowest ebb as ever thou hadst in the greatest flourish and time of prosperity. "Great peace (said the Psalmist) have they that love thy law, and nothing shall offend them" (Psalm 119:165). O happy soul whom no troubles, reproaches, or sufferings are able to offend! Thou mayest meet with prisons, death, banishments, yea, but none of these things shall offend or stumble thee. Thou shalt peaceably and safely pass over them because they are no more than thou expectedst and providest for.

(2.) And by this means thou wilt also prevent the offense and scandals of others at the ways of religion. It is a sad and dangerous thing to be an occasion of stumbling, either to the weak or to the wicked. "Woe to the world because of offenses, for it must needs be that offenses come; but woe to that man by whom the offense cometh" (Matt. 18:7). The apostasies and sinful compliances of ungrounded professors and weak Christians in times of temptation are the woeful occasions of prejudicing others against religion and shedding the blood of souls. Ah! It were much better never to be in the ways of profession than to be there only as a stone of stumbling and a rock of offense to others. All this mischief will be prevented by thy serious expectation of and preparation for the day of evil.

Fourthly, A fourth excellency of preparation for suffering lies in this, that it hath a tendency to convince and awaken the drowsy world. O! If the Lord's people that are providing for a storm resolve, in the strength of God, to run all hazards and hardships for Christ, I am persuaded it would be of more use to startle and convince the world than all the sermons that ever they heard. For here is that which dashes and cuts the throat of all our labors. We preach self-denial, contempt of life, and liberty for Christ. Now, though they hear us preach the necessity and excellency of these things and hear you profess them as your principles, yet when they look upon the lives of professors in times of danger and find no connection between profession and practice; when they see us cling to the world and are as loath to give it up as others; when they observe prisons and sufferings affright and terrify us as much as those that make no profession; when they see us start like hares at every sound and that we live not loose from the world as men prepared to let it go and give it up for Christ, then they conclude that we dare not trust our own principles when it comes to the push. And how can they be persuaded to believe that which they think we ourselves do not really believe, although we persuade them to believe it?

My friends, the world hath eyes to see what you do as well as ears to hear what you say. As long as they see you do no more than others, you may talk your hearts out ere they will believe your way is better than others.

But when persecution arises and they see you preparing yourselves for it by putting on your harness to enter the lists, carrying your dearest enjoyments in your hands, and putting on the shoe of preparation to follow the Lord through the roughest ways of suffering, this preaches the excellency of Christ, the vanity of the creature, and the rationality and certainty of Christian principles in a more intelligible and rousing dialect to them than all our cheap and easy commendations of them did. And hence it is that Noah was said to condemn the world, "By faith Noah being warned by God of things not seen as yet" (Heb. 11:7), that is, of the deluge that was coming, though no appearance of it was yet, the heavens being as clear as ever; yet believing the threatening, "He was moved with fear." The fear of God, an effect of his faith in the word of God, impelled him to his

45

duty, set him about his preparation to provide an ark, and this was it by which he condemned the world and left them excuseless. For they not only heard of an approaching flood by his ministry, but now they saw that he himself believed what he preached by his daily preparations against it. O consider how much it would tend to the world's conviction. Now they will see that you are in good earnest and that there is a reality in godliness. This will induce them to search into the matter more than ever and remove those prejudices they have taken up against the good ways of God as if they were but phantasms and conceits.

Fifthly, In the next place, this foresight and preparation for suffering must needs be an excellent thing because the Spirit of God everywhere sets an honorable character upon it and always mentions such persons with some singular commendation and respect. These only were wise men in the judgment of God, and all the rest (what great politicians so-ever they are famed to be among men) are accounted fools. "The wise man's eyes are in his head" (Pr. 22:3; Eccl. 2:14). That is, he is a foreseeing man, "but the fool goes on, and is punished." He rushes on without consideration, suspecting no danger that he at present sees not and so smarts for his folly. Beloved, there are signs of the times as well as of the weather (Matt. 16:3). You may see the clouds of judgment gathering before the storm falls upon you. And this is the meaning of Zephaniah 2:1-2, "Gather yourselves together before the decree brings forth and the day passes as the chaff." Where there is a conception of judgment, there will be a birth unless the reformations and prayers of the saints cause it to miscarry. But it requires wisdom to discern this. They must be men of great observation that can descry it at a great distance; yet this may be done by considering what God hath done in like cases of former ages when nations have been guilty of the same sins as now they are. For God is as just now as then. He hates sin as much as ever he did, partly by attending to things present, to what fullness and maturity the sins of a nation are grown (Joel 3:16), or what beginnings of judgment are already upon a people, as harbingers and forerunners of more at hand (I Sam 2:12). Or what is the universal note and cry of God's ministers who are his watchmen to foresee danger (Ezek. 3:17) and his trumpeters to discover it (Num. 10:8). And when these have one mouth given them, certainly there is much in it (Lk. 1:70). Or lastly, by pondering those Scripture-prophecies that yet remain to be fulfilled. They must all go out their times and accomplish their full number of years and months, but certainly they shall be fulfilled in their seasons.

By attending to these things, a Christian may give a near guess at the judgments that are approaching a nation and so order himself accordingly. Eccl. 8:5 says, "A wise man's heart discerns both time and judgment." And this is (even in the judgment of God) a choice point of wisdom, whereas, on the contrary, heedless and careless ones that regard not these things are branded for fools and are upbraided with more brutishness than the beasts of the field or fowls of the air (Matt. 16:3). Observe Jeremiah 8:7, "The stork in the heavens, the swallow, turtle, and crane." They observe their seasons of departing and returning upon the approach of the winter and spring, and that by a natural instinct, whereby they prolong their lives which otherwise must perish. But though God hath made man wiser than the fowls of the air and beasts of the earth which by instinct will quit colder climates or run to the hedges when winter or storms approach, yet the heavens may be astonished to see nature cast by sin so far below itself and that in reasonable creatures.

But now, if this be foreseen, then there is a singular advantage in a man's hand to use the means of preventing those approaching calamities. "Seek the Lord all you humble of the earth who have carried out his ordinances; seek righteousness, seek humility. Perhaps you will be hidden in the day of the Lord's anger" (Zeph. 2:3). If it cannot be prevented, he can yet take sanctuary in Christ (Micah 5:5) and run to His promises and attributes to have a good roof over his head while the storm falls and the weather is tempestuous abroad. And therefore, certainly this preparation is an excellent thing. Whatever the Spirit of God speaks in the commendation of foreseeing evils is with respect to this duty of preparing for them, for foresight of evil without preparation increases rather than diminishes the misery.

Sixthly, A sixth excellency of preparation for suffering lies in the influence that it hath into a Christian's stability in the evil day. You cannot but know that your stability in that critical hour of temptation is a choice and singular mercy inasmuch as *all you are worth in the other world depends upon your standing then* (Rev. 21:7; Rom. 2:6,7). Neither can you be ignorant how much you are likely to be tried and put to it, whether with respect to the enemy that engages you (Eph. 6:12) or your own weakness, who have been so often foiled in lesser trials (Jer. 12:5). All the grate[8] you have will be little enough to keep the field and bear you up from sinking. Therefore, it cannot but be a blessed thing to be able to stand and cope with the greatest difficulties in such a time of trial as that will be. "Now he that expects to do this must put on the whole amour of God" (Eph. 6:13). There is no expectation of standing in the evil day except your foot be shod, that is, your wills be prepared with the preparation of the gospel of peace.

It is true that our ability to stand is not from our own inherent grace, "For by his strength shall no man prevail" (I

---

[8] i.e., metal

Sam. 2:9). And yet, it is as true that without grace, both inherent in us and excited and prepared for a storm, we cannot expect to stand. For these two, grace inherent in us and grace exciting and assisting without, are not opposed but coordinated. Grace in us is the weapon by which our enemy falls, but then that weapon must be managed by the hand of the Spirit. Well then, look upon this as a choice mercy which tends so much to your stability.

Seventhly, A seventh excellency of a prepared heart for suffering is that it is a very high testification of our love to Jesus Christ when we thus show our willingness to take our lot with him and follow him wherever he goes. What a high expression of love was that of Ruth to her mother Naomi? "I will not go back, but where thou lodgest I will lodge, and where thou goest I will go." It is excellent when a soul can say to Christ, as Ittai to David in II Samuel 15:21, "Surely in what place my lord the king shall be, whether in death or in life, even there also will thy servant be." This is love indeed, to cleave to him in a time of distresses and dangers. This is "love which the waters cannot quench nor the floods drown" (Song of Solomon 8:7). *Probatio amoris, est exhibitiooperis*, if you love Christ indeed, show your love by some fruits of it. Surely readiness to suffer for Him is a very choice fruit and proof of it. There are many that profess a great deal of love to Christ, but when it comes to this touch-stone, it appears false and counterfeit, just a mere flourish when no danger is near. But that soul which buckles on the shoe of preparation to follow him through thorns and briers, and over rocks and mountains of difficulties and troubles, loves him indeed (Jer. 2:2-3). Beloved, it is one of the choicest discoveries of your love to your master Christ—yea, it is such a testimony of love to him as angels are not capable of. They show their love by their readiness to do his will in the execution of which they fly as

49

with wings (Ezek. 1:24) but you only have the happiness of testifying your love for him by your readiness to suffer for him. Is not this excellent?

Eighthly, When the heart is prepared for the worst suffering, it is an argument that your will is subdued to the will of God—for till this be done, in a good measure, you cannot stand ready to suffer for him. But now, to have the will subdued by grace to the will of God is a very choice and excellent frame indeed, for in this the main power of grace lies. Look in what faculty the chief residence and strength of sin was—now, in the same chief residence the power of grace (after conversion) is also. It is in the will that the strength and power of sin (before conversion) lie (John 5:40; Psalm 30:11; Jer. 44:16-17). And indeed, it was the devil's strong hold, which in the day of Christ's power, Christ stormed and reduced to his obedience (Psalm 110:3). O what a blessed thing is this! The will rules the man—it hath the empire of the whole man. It commands the faculties of the soul, *imperio politico*, and it commands the members of the body, *imperio despotico*. Now to have Christ and grace rule that which rules and commands your inner and outer man is no small mercy. A better evidence that it is so cannot be given than this, that you stand ready or do seriously prepare yourselves to suffer the hardest things for Christ. If your will can like that work, it is an argument grace hath conquered and subdued your will indeed.

Ninthly, This preparation of heart to suffering is an excellent thing because God is so abundantly pleased with it that he often excuses them from suffering in whom he finds it and accepts it as if the service had been actually done. So Abraham (Gen. 22:12) was ready to offer up his Isaac's life to God, but God seeing his servant's heart really prepared and ready for that difficult service and high point of self-denial provided himself another sacrifice instead of Isaac. Abraham shall have his son Isaac back again, and that with advantage, for he hath with him not only a choice experiment of his love to God, but God's high approbation of him and acceptation of his offering. It was all one in respect of divine acceptance, as if he had been slain, and so the Scripture represents it (James 2:21). And in this sense that promise is often made good to God's people who stand ready to give up their Isaacs—that is, their lives, liberties, and dearest enjoyments to the Lord. "He that will lose his life for my name's sake shall save it" (Luke 9:24).

Now what a blessed thing is this! You may in this way have the crown of martyrdom and yet not shed one drop of blood for Christ actually. Ah! How kindly doth God accept it at his poor creatures' hands when he sees how willing they are to serve him with their best enjoyments! "It is well (said he to David) that it was in thy heart" (1 Kings 8:18).

And then, *Lastly*, to add no more, it is beyond controversy an excellent and blessed thing that should such a Christian, after all his pains and preparations, be overborne and fall by temptation, yet this preparation of his heart excuses his fall from those aggravations that are upon the falls of others, and will give him both support under such a condition and encouragement to hope for a speedy recovery out of it. Ah! It is no small comfort when a poor soul that hath been overborne by temptation can come to God and say, "Lord, thou knowest that this was not a willful departure from my duty but contrary to the bent and resolutions of my heart. Thou sawest my diligence beforehand to prepare for it; thou sawest my fears and trembling of heart about it. O Lord, forgive O Lord, recover thy servant and wash away this spot. It is one of the spots of thy children, an infirmity, not a rebellion." This may much stay the soul.

Surely, in this case, thou hast many grounds of comfort that another wants, for thy sin being but an infirmity, for: (1.) It is that which is common to all saints (Psalm 103:11-14); and (2.) God hath mercy and pardon for such sins as these, else woe to the holiest soul (Psalm 130:3-4). Solomon, upon this ground, pled for mercy for them that prepared their hearts (II Chron. 30:18-19). And God hath laid in sweet grounds of encouragement for such souls (Num. 15:27-28; Heb. 5:2). How tenderly doth Christ deal with his disciples under this kind of sin (Matt. 26:41). And though they forsook him for a time, yet he received them again. Though they fled from him, yet they all returned again and appeared boldly for Christ, afterward sealing their confession of him with their blood. And that which recovered them again was that their fall and departure were contrary to the resolution, standing frame, and bent of their hearts, for they all resolved to cleave to him to the death (Matt. 26:35). Whereas those that engaged in a profession of him without counting the cost and who never resolved nor prepared for the worst, fell off from him and never returned anymore (John 6:66). So then, upon the whole you cannot but grant that it is a very blessed and excellent thing to prepare thus for the greatest suffering that can befall us for Christ. We come next to show wherein it lies.

CHAPTER V

The Necessity of a Saving Work of Grace

Acts 21:13 evinces the necessity of a sound and real work of grace upon the heart to fit a man for suffering for Christ.

HAVING showed you that God doth sometimes put his dearest people upon very hard services for him, and what an excellent thing it is to prepare ourselves to obey the call of God to them, in the next place I come to show you wherein this preparation or readiness for suffering consists, and how many things concur and contribute their assistance to this work.

Now, there is a twofold preparation or readiness for suffering—the one is habitual and the other actual. That habitual readiness is nothing else but the inclination of a soul to suffer anything for Christ. This inclination arises from the principles of grace infused into the soul. But then sometimes it is as fire, though it has a natural inclination to ascend, yet it may be violently depressed and hindered so that it cannot ascend actually, as it may be in this case. Therefore, before a man can be fitted for sufferings as Paul was, there must be super-added to this habitual readiness an actual readiness, which is nothing else but the rousing of grace out of the sleepy and dull habits, and awakening it to its work in a time of need. As the lion lashes himself with his tail to rouse up his courage before he fights, so must the Christian. The former is a remote power, the latter is a proximal and immediate power. I must handle the former in this chapter, and you are to know that it consists in a sound and real work of grace or conversion

53

wrought upon the soul, without which I shall make it evidently appear to you that no man can be fit or ready to suffer as a Christian.

Whatever stock of natural courage, moral principles, or common gifts of the Spirit may be lodged in any man's breast, yet all this (without special grace) can never fit him to suffer for Christ. Had not this work been really and soundly wrought upon the heart of this blessed man, as indeed it was (Acts 9:3-6), he would have quickly fainted under his sufferings. Likewise, so will every soul sooner or later that suffers not upon the same principles that he did.

First, No man can suffer for Christ until he be able to deny himself (Matt. 16:24). Self-denial goes in order of nature before sufferings. Beloved, in a suffering hour the interest of Christ and self meet like two men upon a narrow bridge, one must of necessity go back or the other cannot pass on. If you cannot deny self now, you must deny Christ. The yoke and dominion of self must be cast off, or else Christ's yoke and burden cannot be taken on.

It is confessed that self may not only consist with but be a motive to some kind of sufferings. Ambition and applause may carry a man far this way. Pride is a salamander that seems like it could live in the flames of martyrdom (I Cor. 13:3). But to be a servant of self and a true sufferer for Christ is incompatible. Self may make you the devil's martyrs, but only grace can make you Christ's martyrs. So let a man be seemingly carried for a while with never so high a tide of zeal for Christ, yet if self is the spring that feeds those self-ends, it will be like the many little ditches that are joined to the brink of a river which suck and draw away the water into themselves, causing the lofty stream to sink and come to nothing ere it have ran far. So then, of necessity, self must be dethroned in the hearts of Christ's suffering servants.

But now, it is real grace only that disposes self and subjects its interest to Christ's, for sanctification is nothing else but the dethroning of exalted self and the setting up of Christ's interest above it in the soul. This is that which alters the property of all a man hath and super scribes them with a new title, "Holiness to the Lord" (Zech. 14:20-21). Thenceforth a man looks at himself as none of his own but past into another's right (I Cor. 6:19-20) and that he must neither live nor act ultimately for himself but for Christ (Rom. 14:7; Heb. 8:7-8; Phil. 1: 20). He is no more a proprietor but a steward of all he hath, and so he holds upon these terms to lay it out as may best serve his Master's ends and glory.

All that he is or hath is by grace subordinated to Christ. If once subordinated, then no more opposed to him, *subordinata non pugnant*. This is that which makes him say, "I care not what becomes of me, let Christ be glorified." Let Christ be magnified in my body, "whether it be by life or death" (Phil. 1:20).

By conversion, Christ enters the soul as an army doth an enemy's garrison by storm, and when he is possessed of it by grace, he presently divides the whole spoil of self betwixt himself and his church. This is the first thing that evinces the necessity of a work of grace to prepare the heart for sufferings.

Secondly, In the next place, it is evident that a man can never be fit to suffer hard things for Christ until his spirit be enlarged, raised, and ennobled so that he be able to despise dangers and look all difficulties in the face. That low and private spirit must be removed, and a public spirit must possess him. If a man be of a feeble and effeminate spirit, every petty danger will daunt and sink him. Delicacy and tenderness is as unsuitable to a Christian as to a soldier (II Tim. 2:3). They that mean to enter into the kingdom of God must resolve to make their way through that breach of troubles between them and it (II Tim. 3:12). They that will be crowned with victory must stand to it and play the man, as that word imports (I Cor. 16:13). Look over all the sacred and human histories and see if you can find a man that ever honored Christ by suffering who was not of a raised and noble spirit, and in some measure able to contemn[9] both the allurements and threats of men. Take those three noble Jews (Dan. 3:16-17) and Moses (Heb. 11:27) and our apostle (Acts 20:24) for an example. The same heroic and brave spirit was found in the succeeding ages amongst the witnesses of Christ. When Valence, the emperor, endeavored to draw Basil from the faith by offers of worldly rewards, Basil said, "Offer these things [instead] to children." When the emperor threatened Basil with torments, Basil said, "Threaten these things to your purple gallants that live delicately." And the same Basil, relating the story of the forty martyrs said, "When great honors and preferments were offered them to draw them from Christ, their answer was, 'Why offer you these small things of the world to us when you know the whole world is contemned[10] by us?' " The same was true with Luther. Money could not tempt him nor the fear of man daunt him. "Let me (said he in his letter to Staupicius) be accounted guilty of all vices rather than of wicked silence and cowardice in the cause of Christ." Thus you see to what a height and holy greatness the spirits of suffering saints in all ages have been raised.

But now it is grace that thus raises the spirits of men above all the smiles and honors, frowns and fears of men; and no other principle but grace can do it. There is indeed a natural stoutness and generosity in some which may carry them far, as it is said of Alexander, that when any great danger approached

---

[9] i.e., view with contempt
[10] i.e., viewed with contempt

him, his courage would rise and he would say, "*Jam periculum par animo Alexandri*" that is, "Here is a danger fit for Alexander to encounter." So Pompey, when dissuaded from a dangerous voyage, answered, "*Necesse est ut cam, non ut vivam,*" that is, "It is necessary that I go, not that I live." But this being fed only by a natural spring can carry a man no higher than nature and will flag at last. If applause and the observation of the world supply it, it quickly ebbs and fails.

But as grace raises men much higher, so it maintains it even when there is nothing to encourage it without—in particular, even when forsaken of all creatures and visible supports (II Tim. 4:10). It does this in three ways: (1.) By giving him that hath grace a view of far greater things. This view of eternal things, being so high and glorious, shrinks up all temporal things and makes them appear but trifles and small matters (Rom. 8:18; II Cor. 4:18). By grace, a man rises with Christ (Col 3:1). It sets him upon his high places. Thence, he looks down upon things below as very poor and inconsiderable. The great cities of Campania seem but little spots to them that stand on the top of the Alps; (2.) By teaching him to value and measure all things by eternity. He did once measure life, liberty, riches, and honors by sense and time, and then they seemed great things, and it was hard to deny them or thus to slight them. But now he values and measures all by faith and eternity, esteeming nothing great and excellent but what hath a reference to the glory of God and an influence into eternity; (3.) Grace raises and ennobles the spirit thus because it is the divine nature. It is the Spirit of Christ infused into a poor worm which makes a strange alteration on him and transforms him into another manner of person. As much difference betwixt his spirit now and what it was as between the spirit of a child that is filled with small matters and taken up with toys and that of a grave statesman that is daily employed about the grand affairs of a kingdom.

Thirdly, A man can never suffer as a Christian till his will be subjected to the will of God. He that suffers involuntarily and out of necessity, not out of choice, shall neither have acceptance nor reward from God. Of necessity the will must be subjected. A man can never say, "Thy will be done" till he can first say, "Not my will."

But it is grace only that thus conquers and subjects the will of man to God's (Psalm 110:3). This is that which exalts God's authority in the soul and makes the heart stoop and tremble at his commands. It is that which makes our will to write its fiat at the foot of every command and its placet under every order it receives from God. No sooner was grace entered into the soul of Paul but then he cried out, "Lord, what wilt thou have me to do?" (Acts 9:6). The will is to the soul what the wheels are to the chariot, and grace is to the will what oil is to the wheels. When we receive the Spirit of grace, we are said to receive an unction from the Holy One (I John 2:20). And when the soul is made as the chariots of Aminadab (Song of Solomon 6:12) *non tardat uncta rota*, it runs freely after the Lord and cheerfully addresses itself to the very service

Fourthly, A man can never suffer as a Christian until his heart be composed, fixed, and determined to follow the Lord through all hazards and difficulties. As long as a man is hesitating and unresolved what to do, whether to go forward or return back again to the prosperous world, when a man is at such a pause and stand in his way, he is very unfit for sufferings. All such divisions do both weaken the soul and strengthen the temptation. The devil's work is more than half done to his hand in such a soul, and he is now as unfit to endure hardship for Christ as a ship is to ride out a storm that hath neither cable, nor anchor, nor ballast to hold and settle it, but lies at the mercy of every wave. "The double minded man is unstable in all his ways," (James 1:8). But it is grace, and nothing besides, that brings the heart to a fixed resolution and settlement to follow the Lord. It is grace that establishes the heart (Heb. 13:9) and unites it to fear the name of God (Psalm 86:11). This gathers all the streams into one channel, and then it runs with much strength and sweeps away all obstacles before it. So that as with a wicked man that hath sold himself to do wickedly, if he be set upon any one design of sin, he pours out his whole heart and strength into the prosecution of that design, which is the ground of that saying, "*Liberet me Data ab homine unius tantum negotti*," that is, "Let God deliver me from a man of one only design." He will do it to purpose. So is it also in grace—if the heart be composed, fixed, and fully resolved for God, nothing shall then stand before him. And herein lies much of a Christian's habitual fitness and ability to suffer.

Fifthly, The necessity of saving grace in all sufferers for Christ will further appear from the consideration that he who will run all hazards for Christ had need of a continual supply of strength and refreshment from time to time. He must not depend on anything that is fallible; for what shall he do then when that stock is spent and he hath no provision left to live upon? Now all natural qualifications, yea, all the common gifts of the Spirit, are fallible and short-lived things. They are like a sweet flower in the bosom that is an ornament for a little while but withers presently. Or like a pond or brook occasioned by a great fall of rain, which quickly sinks and dries up because it is not fed by springs in the bottom as other fountain-waters are. Hence, it is they cannot continue and hold out when sufferings come (Matt. 13:21) because there is no root to nourish and support. The hypocrite will not always call upon God (Job 27:8-10). Though they may keep company with Christ a few miles in this dirty way, yet they must turn back at last (John 6:66). These comets may seem to shine for a time among the stars, but when that earthly matter is spent, they must fall and lose their glory.

But now grace is an everlasting principle. It hath springs in the bottom that never fail. "I shall be in him," said Christ, "a well of water springing up into eternal life" (John 4:14). The Spirit of God supplies it from time to time, as need requires. It hath daily incomes from heaven (II Cor. 1:5; Phil. 4:18; Col. 1:11). So that it is our union with Christ, the Fountain of Grace, that is the true-ground of our constancy and long suffering. We are only so far safe as we are united to Christ.

And then *Lastly*, it will appear by this also, that there is an absolute necessity of a real change by grace on all that will suffer for Christ because although we may engage ourselves in sufferings without it, yet we can never manage our sufferings like Christians without it. They will neither be honorable nor acceptable to God, nor yet beneficial and comfortable to ourselves or others, except they be performed from this principle of grace. For upon what principle beside this any man is acted in religion, it will either cause him to decline sufferings for Christ, or if he be engaged in them, yet he will little credit religion by his sufferings. They will either be spoiled by an ill management, or his own pride will devour the praise and glory of them. I do not deny but a man that is graceless may suffer many hard things upon the account of his profession and suffer them all in vain as these Scriptures manifest (I Cor. 13:3; Gal. 3:4). Although you may find many sweet promises made to those that suffer for Christ, yet you must consider that those pure and spiritual motives by which men ought to be acted in their sufferings are always supposed and implied in all these promises that are made to the external action. And sometimes it is expressed (I Pet. 4:16). To suffer

60

[as a Christian] is to suffer from pure Christian principles and in a Christian manner, with meekness, patience, and self-denial. And to do so only grace can enable you. So that by all this, I hope what I have undertaken in this character to evince the necessity of a work of grace to pass upon you, before suffering for religion comes, is performed to satisfaction.

61

CHAPTER VI

The Nature of a Saving Work of Grace

Wherein the nature of this work of grace in which our habitual fitness for suffering lies is briefly opened, and an account given of the great advantage the gracious person hath for any suffering, even the hardest work thereby.

HAVING in the former chapter plainly evinced the necessity of saving grace to fit a man for suffering, it will be expected now that some account be given to you of the nature of the work and how it advantages a man for the discharge of the hardest services in religion, both of which I shall open in this chapter by a distinct explication of the parts of the description of it.

This work of grace, of which I am here to speak, consists in the real change of the whole man by the Spirit of God whereby he is prepared for every good work. In a brief description of it, I shall open these four things to you.

First, That it is a change. It is palpably evident, both from Scripture and experience that, "Old things are past away, behold all things are become new" (II Cor. 5:17). It is so sensibly a change that it is called a turning from darkness to light (Acts 26:18) and a new creature formed and brought forth. But to be a little more distinct and particular, there are several other changes that pass upon men which must not be mistaken for this. Therefore, (1.) it is not a mere change of the judgment from error to truth, from Paganism to Christianity. Such a change Simon Magus had, yet he still remained in the gall of bitterness and fast bound in the bonds of iniquity (Acts 8:23); (2.) Nor is it a change only of a man's practice, such as from profaneness to civility. This is common among such as live under the light of the gospel, which breaking into men's consciences, thwarts their lusts and over-awes them with the fears of hell, which is no more than what the Gentiles had (Rom. 2:15); (3.) Nor is it a change from mere morality to mere formality in religion. Thus, hypocrites are changed by the common gifts of the Spirit illuminating their minds and slightly touching their affections (Heb. 6:4-5); (4.) Nor is it such a change as justification makes, which is relative, and only alters the state and condition (Rom. 5:1-2); and lastly, (5.) It is not a change of the essence of a man—he remains essentially the same person still. But this change consists in the infusion of new habits of grace into the old faculties which immediately depose sin from its dominion over the soul and deliver up the soul into the hands and government of Christ so that it lives no more to itself but to Christ. This is that change whereof we speak.

Secondly, And this change I assert to be real—no fancy, no delusion, not a groundless conceit,[11] but it is really existent, *extra mentem*, whether you conceit[12] it or not. Indeed, the blind world would persuade us that the change is merely suppositions and fantastic,[13] and that there is no such real difference betwixt one man and another as we affirm grace makes. And hence, it is that whosoever professes it is presently branded for a fanatic, and that verse Isaiah 65:5, "Stand by thyself, I am holier than thou" clapped in their teeth in their absurd and perverse sense of it.

But I shall briefly offer these seven things to your consideration which will abundantly evince the reality of it and at once both stop the slanderous mouths of ignorant men

---

[11] Belief, something conceived of
[12] i.e., conceive of
[13] fanciful

and silence those atheistical surmises which at any time Satan may inject into the hearts of God's own people touching this matter. And first, (1.) let it be considered that the Spirit of God hath represented to us this work of grace under such names and notions in Scripture as if they had been chosen purposely to obviate this calumny. It is called a new creation (Gal. 6:15), a new man (Eph. 4:24), a new birth (John 3:3), Christ formed in us (Gal. 4:19), all which express its reality and that it is not a conceited[14] thing; (2.) It appears to be real by the marvelous effects it hath upon a man, turning him both in judgment, will, affections, and practice quite counter to what he was before. This is evident in that famous instance of Paul (Gal. 1:23) which is abundantly attested and sealed by the constant experience of all gracious souls that are witnesses of the truth hereof; (3.) A divine and almighty power goes forth to produce and work it. Hence, faith is said to be of the operation of God (Col. 2:12). Yea, that same power which raised Jesus Christ from the dead goes to the production of it (Eph. 1:19, 20). And if so, how much less than blasphemy is it to call it a conceit or fancy? Doth God set on work his infinite power to beget a fancy or raise an imagination? (4.) Conceits[15] and whimsies abound most in men of weak reason. Children and such as are cracked[16] in their understandings have most of them. Strength of reason banishes them as the sun doth mists and vapors. But now, the more rational any gracious person is, the more he is fixed, settled, and satisfied in the grounds of religion. Yea, there is the highest and purest reason in religion, and when this change is wrought upon men, it is carried on in a rational way (Isa. 1:18; John 16:9). The Spirit overpowers the understanding with clear demonstrations and silences all

---

[14] i.e., fanciful notion

[15] i.e., fanciful notion

[16] i.e., broken, immature

objections, pleas, and pretenses to the contrary; (5.) It is a real thing, and gracious souls know it to be so, else so many thousands of the saints would never have suffered so many cruel torments and miseries rather than forsake a fancy and so save all. They have been so well satisfied of the reality of that which the world calls a fancy that they have chosen rather to embrace the stake than deny it. The constancy of Christians in cleaving to religion was common to a proverb among the heathen, who when they would express the greatest difficulty would say, "You may as soon turn a Christian from Christ as do it." Surely no wise man would sacrifice his liberty, estate, life, and all that is dear for a conceit;[17] (6.) Its reality appears in its uniformity in all those in whom it is wrought. They have all obtained like precious faith (II Pet. 1:1). They are all changed into the same image (II Cor. 3:18). Three thousand persons affected in one and the same manner at one sermon (Acts 2:37). Could one and the same conceit possess them altogether? Take two Christians that live a thousand miles distant from each other, that never heard of one another, let these persons be examined and their reports compared, and see if they do not substantially agree, and whether as face answers face in the water, so their experiences do not answer one to the other, which could never be if it were a groundless conceit; (7.) And lastly, it is manifest that it is a reality and puts a real difference betwixt one and another because God carries himself so differently towards them after their conversion— now he smiles, before he frowned; now they are under the promises, before they were under threats and curses. What a vast difference will he put between the one and the other in that great day? (Matt. 25). Surely if these nominal Christians

---

[17] i.e., fanciful notion

66

feels but it spontaneously moves towards him and says, "Stand open ye everlasting gates, that the King of glory may come in." Henceforth, it votes for God, subscribes and submits to his will as its only rule and law, and indeed it becomes the principal seat where grace makes its residence, and where, for the most part, it is more visible than in any other faculty. For after a man hath searched for it in all other faculties and cannot discern it, yet here he ordinarily finds it, to will is present (Rom. 7:18); (3.) The will being thus gained to Christ, love comes in, feeling the power of grace also, and presently changes its object. It seizes not so greedily on earthly objects as before, but is strangely cooled and deadened to them by the appearance of a far greater glory in Jesus Christ, which hath so captivated the soul and strongly attracted their affection that it has now become very remiss in all its actings towards them. And often (especially at first) it is so weaned from all things on earth, that the temptation seems to lie on the other extreme, even in too great neglect of our lawful employments and comforts. Now Jesus Christ (Song of Solomon 1:3), his ordinances, (Psalm 119:97), and his saints (I John 3:14) are the only delights and sweetest companions. He could sit from morning till night to hear discourses of his beloved Christ, and could live and die in the company of Christ's people, whose company is now most delightful and sweet (Psalm 119:63); (4.) Their desires are altered. They pant no more after the dust of the earth (Psalm 4:6) but pant for God as the deer after the water-brooks (Psalm 42:1). Yea, so big is the soul with them that it is sometimes ready to faint, yea, to break with the longing it hath after him (Psalm 119:20); (5.) Their thoughts are changed (Psalm 119:113) and the thoughts of God are now most precious (Psalm 139:17) musing when alone of him; and in its solitudes the soul entertains itself with a delightful feast, which its thoughts of God bring in to refresh it (Psalm 63:5-6);

68

(6.) The designs and projects of the soul are changed, being swallowed up in one grand design—namely, to approve himself to God and be accepted of him (II Cor. 5:9). If he fails not there, it will not much trouble him if all his other designs should be dashed. It were easy to instance in the rest of the affections and show how grace spreads and diffuses itself into them all as light in the air or leaven in the lump, but this may suffice to show how it passes upon the whole soul and enters the several faculties and affections thereof.

And the soul being thus possessed for God, the body with all its members is consequently resigned up to him also. For the will hath the empire of the manners of the body as well as of the passions and affections of the soul. These are not any more delivered up to execute the lusts of Satan but are yielded up to God for his ends and uses (Rom. 6:19). And thus, you have the third thing in the description made out also, that it is a universal as well as a real change. But then,

Fourthly, You must know that by this change God prepares a man for choice and excellent service, and this indeed is the main thing designed in this chapter. It is the result and issue of all that hath hitherto been said about this work of grace.

Beloved, can you imagine that God could employ his infinite and glorious power to produce this new creature in such an excellent nature, it being the master-piece of all his works of wonder wrought upon man, and not aim at some singular use and excellent end? Every wise agent designs some end, and what God aims at he hath told us (Isa. 43:21; Eph. 2:10). And accordingly he expects singular things from such persons (Matt. 5:47). If God had not aimed at some new service, he need not have made a new creature—the old creature was fit enough for the old use and service it was employed in. But God hath some choice service to be done wherein he will be glorified. He will have his name glorified,

69

even in this world, by the active and passive obedience of his people. But this being far above all the power of nature, God therefore brings them forth in a new and heavenly nature, endowed with rare, supernatural, and divine qualities, by which it is fitted and excellently prepared for any service of God, by doing or suffering that which before he had no fitness or ability.

The very make and constitution of this new creature speaks its use and end. As now, if a man look upon a sword or knife, (supposing he had never seen either before) yet, I say, by viewing the shape and properties of it, he will say, this was made to cut. Even so, this new creature was formed for some glorious and singular service for God to which it is exceedingly advantaged, whether God put you upon doing or suffering. If you ask wherein this advantage of the new creature to honor God either way lies, I answer, it principally consists in its heavenly inclination or natural tendency to God. This is its great advantage, for, by virtue of this,

First, If God calls a man to any duty, there is a principle within closing with the command without and moving the soul freely and spontaneously to duty (Psalm 27:8). If God says, "Seek my face," such a heart echoes to the call, "Thy face, Lord, will I seek." And this is it which is called, "The writing of God's law in the heart" (Jer. 31:33). This must needs be a mighty advantage, for now its work is its delight and wages (Psalm 19:11). The command to such a soul is not grievous (I John 5:3) and by this it is kept from tiring in duty and being weary of its work. As you see what pains children can take at play—how they will run and sweat, and endure knocks and falls, and take no notice of it; but put them upon any manual labor, and they cannot endure half so much. When our work is our delight, we never faint nor tire at it. This inclination to God is to the soul as wings to a bird or sails to a ship. This

70

carries the soul easily through every duty. O there is a vast difference between a man that works for wages and one whose work is wages to him. And here you may at once see wherein the principal difference between the hypocrite and real Christian lies in the performance of duty. This also gives a true account of the reason why one perseveres in his work to the end when the other flags. Why, here is the true account of both—the one is moved to duty from a natural inclination to it, while the other is forced upon it by some external motives. For the hypocrite takes not delight in the spiritual and inward part of duty but is secretly weary of it (Mal. 1:13). Only his ambition and self-ends put him upon it is as a task. But now the upright heart goes to God as his joy (Psalm 63:4) and says, "It is good for me to draw nigh to God" (Psalm 73:28). When the Sabbath comes (that golden spot of the week), O how he longs to see the beauty of the Lord in his ordinances! (Psalm 27:4). And when engaged in the worship of God, he cannot satisfy himself in bodily service or serve God in the oldness of the letter. He knows that the persuasion to do so comes not of him that called (Gal. 5:7-8). He labors to engage his heart to approach to God (Jer. 30:21). Hence, those mountings of heart and violent sallies of the desires are heavenward. Thus, you see one rare advantage to glorify God actively flowing from the inclination of this new creature.

Secondly, in like manner, the soul hath a great advantage for suffering, for this new creature, having such a natural tendency to God, will enable the soul in which it is to break its way to God through all the interposing obstacles and discouragements. What are persecutions, what are reproaches, what are the fears and frowns of enemies but so many blocks thrown into the soul's way to keep it from God and duty? And indeed, where this principle of grace is wanting, they prove inaccessible mountains. Graceless hearts are stalled and quite

71

thereby enabling them sensibly to see and feel it to their own satisfaction. And this is expressed in Scripture under a pleasant variety of metaphors. Sometimes it is called the "shedding abroad of the love of God in the heart" (Rom. 5:5). Sometimes it is called "the lifting up of the light of God's countenance" (Psalm 4:6). Sometimes it is expressed without a trope by Christ's manifesting himself to the soul (John 14:21). For the opening of it, I desire you would consider these six things: (1.) That it is attainable by believers in this life and that in a very high degree and measure. Many of the saints have had it in a full measure (I Cor. 2:12; John 3:29-30; 21:15); (2.) Though it be attainable by believers, yet it is a thing separable from true grace, and many precious souls have gone mourning for the want of it. This was sometimes the case of Heman, David, Job, and multitudes more; (3.) During its continuance, it is the sweetest thing in the world. It swallows up all troubles and doubles all other comforts. It puts more gladness into the heart than the increase of corn and wine (Psalm 4:7). *Suavis hora, sed brevis mora; sapit quidem suavissime sed gustatur rarissime*; (4.) Both in the continuation and removal of it the Spirit acts arbitrarily. No man can say how long he shall walk in this pleasant light. "By thy favor, thou hast made my mountain stand strong. Thou hidest thy face, and I was troubled" (Psalm 30:7). And when in darkness, none can say how long it will ere be till the sweet light will break forth again. God can scatter the cloud unexpectedly in a moment. "It was but a little that I passed from them, but I found him whom my soul loveth" (Song of Solomon 3:4). There is such an observable difference in David's spirit in some psalms, as if one man had written the beginning, and another, the end; (5.) Though God can quickly remove the darkness and doubts of a soul, yet ordinarily the saints find it a very hard and difficult thing to obtain and preserve the evidences of their graces.

Secondly, I shall show you the advantage of it to a suffering saint in order to the right management of a suffering condition. And this will appear by the consideration of five things: (1.) You will readily grant that the Christian's love to God hath a mighty influence into all his sufferings for God. This grace of love enables him to victoriously break through all difficulties and discouragements. "The floods cannot drown it, nor the waters quench it" (Song of Solomon 8:6-7). It facilitates the greatest hardships (I John 5:3). And whatever a man suffers, if it be not from this principle, it is neither acceptable to God nor available to himself (I Cor. 13:3). But now, nothing more inflames and quickens the Christian's love to God than the knowledge of God's interest in him and the sensible perception and taste of his love to the soul. Our love to God is but a reflection of his own love; and the more powerful the stroke of the direct beam, the more is that of the reflex beam also. Never doth that flame of Yahweh burn with a more vehement heat than when the soul hath the most clear manifestations of its interest in Christ and his benefits (Luke 7:47); (2.) It must needs be of singular use to a suffering saint because it takes out the sinking weight of affliction. That which sinks and breaks the spirit is the conjunction and meeting of inward and outward troubles together. Then, if the Lord does not strangely and extraordinarily support the soul, it is wrecked and overwhelmed, as the ship in which Paul sailed when it fell into a place where two seas met (Acts 27:41). O how tempestuous a sea doth that soul fall in that hath fightings without and fears within! How must that poor Christian's heart tremble and meditate terror, for when he retires from troubles without for some comfort and support within, there he finds a sad addition to his troubles from whence he expected relief against them! Hence, it was that Jeremiah so earnestly deprecates such a misery, "Be not thou a terror to me, thou art my hope in the day of evil" (Jer. 17:17). This is prevented by this means—if a man has a clear breast and all be quiet within, he is like one that hath a good roof over his head when the storm falls. "We glory in tribulation, because the law of God is shed abroad in our hearts" (Rom. 5:3, 5); (3.) It is a fountain of joy and comfort in the darkest and saddest hour—hence, the glorious triumphs of saints in their afflictions (Rom. 5:5). And in the joy in the Lord lies much strength for sufferings (Neh. 8:10). Once the spirit droops and sinks, the man is in a bad case to suffer. Holy joy is the oil that makes the chariot-wheels of the soul free to follow the Lord, *Non tardat uncta rota*. To suffer with joyfulness for Christ is a qualification that God's eye is much upon in his suffering servants (Col. 1:11). How did the famous worthies that went before us magnify Christ and glorify religion by the holy triumphs of their faith and joy under tribulation! One kissed the apparitor that brought him news of his condemnation and was like a man transported with an excess of joy. Another, upon the pronouncing of the sentence, knelt down, and with hands and eyes lifted up, solemnly blessed God for such a day. Oh how is Christ magnified by this! And this cannot be until an interest in Christ is cleared. It is true, the faith of recumbency[20] gives the soul a secret support and enables the Christian to live; but the faith of evidence keeps him lively and prevents all those uncomfortable and uncomely sinkings and despondencies of spirit (II Cor. 4:16-17). Therefore, it cannot but be of a singular use to a soul at such a time; (4.) And, lastly, it is of special use to a Christian under suffering, inasmuch as it enables him to repel the temptations that attend upon sufferings. Nothing sets a keener edge upon his indignation against unworthy compliances than this. Indeed, a poor,

---

[20] .i.e., resting in the Lord and His truth

cloudy, and dubious Christian will be apt to catch at deliverance,[21] though upon terms dishonourable to Christ; but he that is clear in point of interest abhors compositions and capitulations upon unworthy terms and conditions (Heb. 10:34; 11:35). He that sees the gain and reward of suffering will think he is offered loss when life and deliverance are set before him upon such hard terms as sin is. And thus, you see what influence it hath into a suffering condition.

Thirdly, In the next place, I promised to prescribe some rules for the attaining of this evidence and the dispelling of those doubts by which it is usually clouded in the souls of believers. And oh, that by the faithful use of them you may attain it when a suffering day comes upon you.

1. Rule: And the first rule I shall give you is this—make it your business to improve grace more, for the more *vigorous* it is, the more *evidential* it will need be (II Pet. 1:5-11). O how much time have many Christians spent in inquiring after the lowest signs of sincerity[22] and what may consist with grace? O if only they had spent that time in the diligent improvements of the means of grace and for the increasing of it, they would have found it a short-cut to peace and comfort by much.

2. Rule: Mistake not the rule by which you are to try yourselves lest you give a false judgment upon yourselves. Some are apt to make those things signs of grace which are not; and when the falseness of them is detected, how is that poor soul plunged into doubts and fears that leaned upon them? As now, if a man should conclude his sincerity from his diligence in attending on the word preached, this is but a

---

[21] That is, find a way to deliver himself out of the suffering

[22] i.e., inquiring how far one can push the limits of Christian freedom and still be a "Christian".

thou fall short of it in thy practice (Rom. 7:12, 14). (b.) If thy failings be involuntary and against the resolution and bent of thy soul (Rom. 7:15, 18, 19). (c.) If it be the load and burden of thy soul when you fail God's law (Rom. 7:24). (d.) If the thoughts of deliverance from sin comfort thee (Rom. 7:25); (2.) Question not the truth of thy grace because it was not wrought in the same way and manner in thee as in others. For there is a great variety as to the circumstances of time and manner between the Spirit's operations in one and another. Compare the history of Paul's conversion with that of the Philippian jailor, Zaccheus, or Lydia, and see the variety of circumstances; (3.) Conclude not that you have no grace because you feel not those transports and ravishing joys that other Christians speak of. If thou canst not say as Paul doth (Rom. 8:38), yet bless God if thou canst but breathe forth such language as that in Mark 9:24, "Lord, I believe, help thou my unbelief"; (4.) Say not thou hast no grace because of the high attainments of some hypocrites who in some things may excel thee. When some persons read the sixth chapter to the Hebrews, they are startled to see what a glorious height the hypocrite may soar, not considering that there are these three things wherein they excel the most glorious hypocrite in the world: (a.) That self was never dethroned in hypocrites, as it is in them. All that a hypocrite doth is for himself. (b.) The hypocrite never hated every sin as he doth, but hath still some Agag, Rimmon, or Delilah. (c.) The hypocrite never acts in duty from the bent and inclination of a new nature by taking delight in heavenly employment, but is moved rather as a clock by the weight and poises of some external motives and advantages; (5.) Conclude not that you have no grace because you grow not as sensibly as some other Christians do. You may be mistaken in divers ways about this if you: (a.) Measure your growth by your desires, and then it appears nothing, for the Christian aims high and grasps at all. (b.) Or by comparing yourselves with such as have larger capacities, time, and advantages than you. (c.) Or by comparing your graces with other men's gifts which you mistake for their graces. (d.) Or by thinking that all growth is upward in joy, peace, and comfort, whereas you may grow in mortification and humility, which is as much a growth as the former. Oh, take heed of these mistakes that have been very prejudicial to the peace of many Christians.

5. Rule: Lastly, do not decline sufferings when God gives you a fair call to them. Oh! The Christian's suffering time is commonly his clearest and most comfortable time! "Then the Spirit of God and glory rests on them" (I Pet. 4:14). That which hath been in suspense for some years is decided and cleared in a suffering hour. And thus, I have shown you how to attain this necessary qualification also.

CHAPTER VIII

The Necessity of Improving Faith

Discovering the necessity of an improved faith for the right management of suffering and directing to some special means for the improvement thereof.

THE next thing conducing to our actual readiness for suffering is the improvement of faith to some considerable degree of strength. This is the grace that must do the main service in such an hour and hath the principal hand in supporting the Christian under every burden. This is the grace that crowns our heads with victory in the day of battle. "Above all taking the shield of faith" (Eph. 6:16). It is true every grace is of use and contributes assistance. Suffering saints have been beholding to them all. But of this we may say, as Solomon said of the virtuous woman, "Though many graces have done excellently, yet this excels them all." In this grace Paul was very eminent; it was the life he daily lived (Gal. 2:20). Oh! It is a precious grace (II Pet. 1:1). It is so precious that Christ, who seldom admired anything, wondered at it (Matt. 8:10). A victorious grace it is that overcomes all difficulties (Mark 9:23). By this sword, it was that all those famous heroes in Hebrews 11 achieved all those glorious conquests, and in every distress it may say to the soul, as Christ to the disciples, "Without me ye can do nothing" (John 15:5). This is that sword that hath obtained so many victories over the world (I John 5:4). And it is that trusty shield that hath quenched so many deadly darts of temptation which have been leveled at the very heart of a Christian in the day of battle. By it a Christian lives when all outward, sensible comforts die (Hab.

2:4). It is the ground upon which the Christian fixes his foot and never fails under him (II Cor. 1:24). The necessity of it will more clearly appear by considering how many ways it relieves the soul in trouble and disburdens the heart of all its sinking loads and pressures. There are two things that sink a man's spirit when under sufferings: (1.) the greatness of the troubles; and (2.) the weakness of the soul to bear them. Faith relieves the soul against both by making a weak soul strong and heavy troubles light.

First, Faith makes a weak soul strong and able to bear, and this it doth by divers ways. (1.) It does it by purging out of the soul those enfeebling and weakening distempers—not only *guilt* in general, which is to the soul as a wound upon the bearing shoulder (Rom. 5:1) and the removal whereof enables the soul to bear any other burden, but it does it also by removing *fear*, that tyrant passion that cuts the nerves of the soul. For as faith comes in, so fear goes out. Look in what degree the fear of God is ascendant in the soul, and proportionally the sinful fear of the creature declines and vanishes (Isa. 8:12-13). This godly fear extinguishes sinful fear as sunshine puts out fire. "The righteous is bold as a lion" (Prov. 28:1). The Hebrew word *kephiyr* in this verse signifies a young lion in his hot blood that knows no such thing as fear! And look, however much of the soul is empty of faith, is filled with fear. "Why are ye fearful, O ye of little faith?" (Matt. 8:26). Certainly, it is a rare advantage to be freed from the common distraction in times of common destruction, and this advantage the soul hath by faith. (2.) Faith strengthens the soul to bear afflictions and hardships not only by purging out its weakening distempers, but also by turning itself to Christ, in whom all its strength lies, and that suitably to the several needs of the soul in all its distresses. Doth darkness, like the shadow of death, overspread the earth and all the lights of

84

earthly comforts disappear? Then faith supports the heart by looking to the Lord (Micah 7:7). And this look of faith exceedingly revives the heart (Psalm 34:5) and enlightens the soul. Doth God pluck away all earthly props from under your feet and leave you nothing visible to rest upon? In that need faith puts forth a suitable act by resting or staying upon God (Isa. 26:3), and by this the soul comes to be quieted and established (Psalm 125:1). Do temptations strive to put off the soul from Christ and discourage it from leaning upon the promise? Then faith puts forth an act of resolution (Job 13:15). And so faith breaks its way through that discouragement. Hath the soul been long seeking God for deliverance out of trouble, and still there is silence in heaven and no answer comes—and instead of an answer comes a temptation to throw up the duty and seek to deliver itself? Then faith puts forth another act upon Christ suitable to this distress by an act of waiting (Isa. 49:23); and this waiting on the Lord is opposed to that sinful haste which the soul is tempted to (Isa. 28:16). Or doth God at any time call the soul forth to some difficult service against which the flesh and carnal reason dispute and plead? Now faith helps the soul by putting forth an act of obedience and that whilst carnal reason stands by dissatisfied (Gal. 1:16). And hence, it is that obedience carries the name of faith upon it to show its descent (Rom. 16:26). Faith encourages the soul to obey, not only by urging God's command, but by giving it God's warrant for its indemnity[23] (Heb. 11:24-26). Or doth a poor believer find himself overmatched by troubles and temptations, and his own inherent strength begun to tail under the burden? Then faith leads him to an omnipotent God and so secures him from fainting under his trouble (Psalm 61:2). In the Lord is everlasting strength. El Shaddai is a name of

---

[23] i.e., compensation, reward

85

encouragement to a feeble soul (Isa. 40:29-31). And thus, you see the first particular made good by what a strengthening influence faith hath upon a weak soul.

Secondly, In the next place, let us see how it lightens the Christian's burdens as well as strengthens his back to bear. And certainly, this grace of faith doth strangely alter the very nature of suffering, taking away both the heaviness and horror of it, and this it doth divers ways.

1. By committing the business to Christ and leaving the matter with him, and so quitting the soul of all these anxieties and perturbations which are the very burden and weight of affliction (Psalm 37:5). For certainly that which sinks us in days of trouble is rather from within—from our unruly, seditious, and clamorous thoughts rather than from the troubles themselves with which we conflict. But by committing the matter to God, the soul is quickly brought to rest.

2. By discovering much present good in our troubles. The more good faith discovers in a trouble, the more supportable and easy it makes it to the soul. Now faith brings in a comfortable report that sufferings are not only evils, as the troubles of the wicked are (Ezek. 7:5), but have an allay and mixture of much good (Heb. 12:10; Isa.27:9).

3. By foreseeing the end and final removal of them, and that near at hand (II Cor. 4:17). That which daunts and amazes men in times of trouble is that they can see no end of them. Hence, the heart faints and hands hang down through discouragement. But now faith brings the joyful tidings of the end of troubles and says to the soul, "Why art thou cast down, O my soul? And why so disquieted and discouraged within

me?" (Psalm 42:5) as if thy sufferings were like the sufferings of the damned, endless and everlasting, whereas they are but for a moment. Yet in a little while, a very little while, "he that shall come will come and will not tarry" (Heb. 10:37). Yet a little while, and then the days of thy mourning shall be over.

4. By comparing our sufferings with the sufferings of others, which exceedingly diminishes and shrinks them up. Sometimes the believer compares his sufferings with Christ's and then he is ashamed that ever he should complain and droop under them. "Oh!" said he, "What is that to that which the Lord Jesus suffered for me? He suffered in all his members—head, hands, side, and feet from all friends and enemies, in all his offices; yea, in his soul, as well as in his body. And indeed, the sufferings of his soul were the very soul of his sufferings." Sometimes he compares them with the sufferings of other saints in former ages. When he reads in faith the history of their persecutions, he is ashamed of his complaints and says, "Am I better than my fathers?" Sometimes he compares them with the suffering of the damned. "O what is this to everlasting burning! What is a prison to hell? How light and easy is it to suffer for Christ in comparison with those sufferings of Christ?" And thus the soul is quieted and the terror of suffering abated.

5. Faith entitles Christ to the believer's suffering and puts them upon his score, and so it exceedingly transforms and alters them. Ah! It is no small relief when a man can hold up the Bible, as that martyr did at the stake, and say, "This is that which hath brought me hither." Or as the psalmist, "For thy sake we are killed all the day long." Or as the apostle in Colossians 1:24, "I fill up that which is lacking in the sufferings of Christ in my flesh."

87

6. Lastly, Faith engages the presence of God to abide with the soul in all its solitudes and sufferings. It lays hold upon the promises made to that purpose (Psalm 23:2; Isa. 43:2; Heb. 13:5; John 14:18). And whilst a poor soul enjoys this, the very sense of troubles is swallowed up.

And thus, I have given some brief hints how faith relieves and strengthens the soul in a suffering hour. The next thing is to direct you how to improve this excellent grace that it may do you such service as this in a time of need. And, in order thereunto, I shall give you these seven directions.

1. Attend diligently upon the ministration[24] of the gospel, which is not only the procreant[25] but also the conserving[26] cause of faith (I Pet. 2:2). *The doctrine of faith is the food and nutrient of the grace of faith.* There are its rules, its encouragements, and its cordials. Thence, faith takes and treasures up its michtams[27] to which it hath recourse in times of need. Every attribute, command, or promise that shines forth in Scripture is a dish for faith to feed on, but all together they are a royal feast (Psalm 63:5). Some say the land of Judea is called the land of the living in Psalm 27:13 because of the ordinances of God which that people enjoyed. Certainly it is. God's ordinances are the great instruments of quickening souls

---

[24] i.e., the ministry of the gospel, such as attending to preaching, corporate worship, and teaching

[25] i.e., regenerating

[26] i.e., preserving

[27] writing; i.e., a poem or song found in the titles of Psalms 16, 56-60. Some translate the word "golden", i.e., precious. It is rendered in the LXX by a word meaning "tablet inscription" or a "stelograph." The root of the word means to stamp or grave, and hence it is regarded as denoting a composition so precious as to be worthy to be engraven on a durable tablet for preservation; or, as others render, "a psalm precious as stamped gold," from the word _kethem_, "fine or stamped gold." *Easton's Bible Dictionary*, www.dictionary.com

In this context, treasuring up faith's michtam's may refer to engraving or hiding God's Word upon the heart through study, meditation and memorization.

at first and of preserving that life it so begat in them. But then be sure they have Christ's stamp upon them and that they be ministered by his own officers and in his own way. And so, you may reasonably expect more fruits and influences from them than from all private gifts and helps in the world. "For the Lord loveth the gates of Zion more than all the dwellings of Jacob" (Psalm 87:2). And all private helps may say, in comparison of Christ's public ordinances, as Gideon said to the men of Ephraim in Judges 8:2, "What have we done in comparison to you?"

2. Improve well your sacrament seasons[28]—those harvest days of faith. This ordinance hath a direct and peculiar tendency to the improvement and strengthening of faith. It is a pledge superadded to the promise for faith's sake. Heavenly and sublime mysteries do therein stoop down to your senses that you may have the clearer apprehensions of them—and the clearer the apprehensions are, the stronger the assent of faith must needs be. By this seal also the promise comes to be more ratified to us; the firmer the promise appears to the soul, the more bold and adventurous faith is in casting itself upon it. Oh! How many poor, doubting, trembling souls have (in such a season) gathered the full ripe fruits of assurance from the top-boughs of that ordinance!

3. Frequent actings of faith are rare and special means of improving it. To him that hath, i.e., that improves and uses what he hath, shall be given more (Matt. 25:29). "Stand open ye everlasting gates, that the King of glory may come in" (Psalm 24:7). This was the way by which Paul thrived in faith and every other grace so exceedingly that he outgrew them

---

[28] i.e., the Lord's Supper

that were in Christ before him (I Cor. 15:10). It is true that its beginning in the soul is not after the manner of other habits, either moral or natural. This is not of natural acquisition, but by divine infusion. Yet its improvement is in the same manner. Oh then, if ever you would have a flourishing faith, rouse it up out of the dull habit and live in the daily exercise of it.

4. Go to Jesus Christ, who is the author and finisher of faith, and cry to him, as in Mark 9:24, "Lord, increase my faith." Yea, beg the assistance of others to pray this on your behalf, as the apostle did in I Thessalonians 3:10 and II Thessalonians 1:11. Faith animates prayer, and prayer increases faith.

5. Improve times of affliction for the increase of faith. Certainly, sanctified afflictions do notably exercise and increase this grace (I Pet. 1:7). In times of prosperity we know not what stock of faith we have—we live so much upon things seen that we cannot many times tell whether we have faith or not. But when difficult days come, then we must get out our whole subsistence and livelihood by faith (Hab. 2:4). Yea, then we have many proofs and experiments of God's fidelity in the promises which is a choice help to faith (II Cor. 1:10).

6. Keep catalogues of all your remarkable experiences and treasure them up as food to your faith for times to come. Oh! It is a singular encouragement and heartening to faith when it can turn over the records of God's dealing with you in years past and say as Joshua, "Not one promise of God's hath failed" (Joshua 23:14). When it can say so of promises that have already had their accomplishments, then they will be apt to say concerning those yet to be accomplished, as Elisabeth said to Mary in Luke 1:45, "Blessed is the soul that believeth, for there shall be a performance of those things which are told

it by the Lord." These experiments are the food of faith. "Thou breakest the heads of Leviathan in pieces and gavest him to be meat to thy people inhabiting the wilderness" (Psalm 74:14). That famous experience of the power and love of God in their Red-sea deliverance, where he destroyed that sea-monster Pharaoh and his host, was meat to the faith of God's Israel in the wilderness afterward. We often find Christ charging the people's unbelief on a bad memory (Matt 16:8-9). And hence, it was that the Lord commanded the Israelites to keep journals of every day's occurrences. It is a thousand pities such choice helps should be lost. Oh! If you could but remember how the Lord hath appeared for you in former exigencies[29] and how often he hath shamed you for your unbelief, it would exceedingly animate your faith, both in present and future distresses (Micah 6:5).

7. Lastly, beware of sense, which is the supplanter of faith. O if you live upon earthly things, you put your faith out of its office. Things earthly have an enmity to faith. "This is the victory by which we overcome the world, even our faith" (I John 5:4). Overcoming denotes a conflict, and conflicts infer oppositions. Oh, you that live so much by sight and sense on things visible, what will you do when in David's or Paul's case (Psalm 142:4; II Tim. 4:16) all outward encouragements and stays shall utterly fail? What had Abraham done if he had not been able to believe against hope, that is, the kind of hope that is founded on sense and reason and not faith.

Reader, I advise and charge thee in the name of the Lord and as thou hopest to live when visible comforts die, that thou be diligent in the improvement and preparation of this excellent grace of faith. If it fail, thou failest with it. As thy

---

[29] i.e., times of need or emergencies

CHAPTER IX

The Necessity of Christian Fortitude

Wherein the necessity and usefulness of Christian fortitude in order to suffer is proven, with a brief account of its nature and the means of attaining it.

THE next grace which occurs to the completing of our actual readiness for suffering is Christian fortitude or holy courage, which must say in the heart in time of danger, as Elijah once did, "As the Lord of hosts lives, before whom I stand, I will show myself to him [i.e., King Ahab] today" (I Kings 18:15). This also is a choice part of your preparation-work. In this grace our apostle was eminent. When he was told that "bonds and afflictions" awaited him, he could say that "none of these things moved him" (Acts 20:24). Yea, when he was to appear before the lion Nero, and not a man would own or stand by him, yet he stood his ground, resolving rather to die on the place than to dishonorably recede from his principles and profession (II Tim. 4:16-17). He set the world, with all its threats and terrors, lower than it set him. O how conspicuous was this grace in all those heroes that have past on before us. If ever you hope to stand in the evil day and be fetched off the field with honor, you must rouse up and awaken your courage for God. And the necessity thereof will appear upon these four considerations.

1. Because the success and prevalence of Satan's temptations in the hour of persecution depends upon the fainting and overthrow of this grace. Wherefore doth he raise persecutions in the world but because such terrible things are fitted to work

upon the passion of carnal fear, which rises with those dangers and makes the soul as a tumultuous sea. This is what he aims at. Nehemiah 6:13, "He was hired for this reason, that I might become frightened and act accordingly and sin." This is a multiplying passion that represents dangers more and greater than they are, and so drives the soul into the very net and snare laid by the devil to take it. "The fear of man brings a snare" (Prov. 29:25) which was sadly exemplified in Abraham (Gen. 12:12) and divers others of the saints. If he can but subdue this grace, he will quickly bring you to capitulate for life and liberty upon the basest and most dishonorable terms. Therefore, the preparation of this grace is so exceedingly necessary.

2. Because this is the grace that honors Jesus Christ abundantly when you are brought upon the stage for him. There is a great solemnity at the suffering and trial of a saint. Heaven, earth, and hell are spectators observing the issue and how the saints will acquit themselves in that hour. "We are made a spectacle" said the apostle (I Cor. 4:9). The word is Θεατρον εγενηθημεν, *theatron egenathamen,* we are as set upon a theatre in public view. God, angels, and saints wait to see the glorious triumphs of their faith and courage, reflecting honor upon the name and cause of Christ. Devils and wicked men gape for an advantage by their cowardice. Certainly very much lies now upon the Christian's hands. Should he faint and give ground, how will it furnish the triumphs of hell and make Christ's enemies vaunt over him, as if his love ran so low in the hearts of his people that they durst not adventure anything for him? Or, as if notwithstanding their brave words and glorious profession, they durst not trust their own principles when it comes to the trial. But if now they play the man and discover a holy gallantry of spirit and resolution for Christ,

how will it daunt the enemies and make them say (as Marcus, bishop of Aretheusa made one of Julian's nobles present at his torments to say concerning him), "We are ashamed, O emperor, the Christians laugh at thy cruelty!" How will God himself rejoice and glory over them as he once did over Job when he fetched him with honor off that first field, "Still he holds fast his integrity" (Job 2:3).

3. Your own peace is wrapped up in it, as well as God's glory. Is it nothing, think you, to be freed from those vultures and harpies that feed upon the hearts of men at such times? Surely God reckons that he promises a very great mercy to his people when he promises it (Psalm 112:7). When Borromaeus was told of some that lay in wait to take away his life, it troubled him not, but he said, "*An Deus est in mundo pro nihilo?*" meaning, "What, is God in the world for naught?" And to this was the answer of Silentiarius in the like case, "*Si Deus mei curam non habet, quid vivo?*" namely, "If God take not care for me, how do I live?" Oh, this is that which brings you to a holy quietude of spirit in times of confusion and distraction, which is a choice mercy.

4. Your magnanimity is of special use to other saints who are following you in the same path of sufferings. If you faint, it is like the fainting of a standard-bearer in an army—you bring thereby an evil report upon the cross of Christ as the first spies did upon the land of Canaan. And a similar influence it is likely to have on your brethren, so that there is a necessity of improving this grace also before you can say with Paul that you are ready.

But what is this Christian fortitude and wherein doth it consist? I answer briefly—it is a holy boldness in the performance of difficult duties, flowing from faith in the call of God and his promise to us in the discharge of them. And so you have the nature of it in these four particulars.

1. It is a holy boldness, not a natural or sinful boldness arising either from the natural constitution or evil disposition of the mind.

2. It is expressed about duties for truth, not error (Jer. 9:3), for the interest of Christ, not of the flesh.

3. The season in which it appears is when duties are surrounded and beset with difficulties and dangers (Dan. 3:16-18; 6:10).

4. The fountain whence it flows is faith, and that as it respects the command and call of God to duty (Acts 16:10) and his promise to us in the discharge thereof (Josh. 1:5-6). And his grace stands opposed both to the fear of man in the cause of God (Heb. 11:27) and to apostasy from the truth for fear of suffering. Thus, briefly of the nature of it.

5. In the last place, I shall lay down some rules for the promoting and improvement of it and so finish this chapter. Now there are ten rules heedfully to be observed for the breeding of holy courage in the breast of a saint in evil times.

1. Rule: The first rule is get a weaned heart from all earthly enjoyments. If the heart be inordinately fixed upon any one thing that you possess in the world, that inordinate estimation of and affection for it will strangely effeminate, soften, and cowardize your spirit when your trial comes (II Tim. 2:4). You meet not with a man of courage for God but whose heart is

dead to earthly things, as it was with Paul (Phil. 3:8). Since the apostles, we scarce meet with a greater example of magnanimity than Luther. If you have read his story, you will find few men ever set a lower rate on the world than he. All the Turkish empire in his eyes was but a crumb cast to the dogs. *Germana est haec bestia pecunium non curat*. Money could not tempt him.

2. Rule: Suffer not guilt to lie upon your consciences—it is a fountain of fears, and you can never attain boldness for God till it be removed (Rom. 5:1-3). The spirit of a sound mind is opposed to the spirit of fear (II Tim. 1:7). Now that sound mind is a mind or spirit that is not wounded and made sick by guilt. O what black fogs and mists arise out of guilt which becloud our evidences and fill us with fear and discouragements (Gen. 42:21-22).

3. Rule: Clear your call to difficult services. Be well satisfied that you are in that way and posture that God expects to find you in. O what courage this will give! (Josh. 1:9). Then a man may promise himself God's presence and protection (II Chron. 15:2). But whilst a man is dubious here and cannot tell whether it be his duty or not that he is engaging in, how can he have courage to hazard anything for it? For he thinks, "I may suffer much from men, and yet have no thanks of God for it." And further, till a man be clear in this, he cannot commit his cause to God. And it is a sad thing to be cut off from so choice a relief as that is (I Pet. 4:19).

4. Rule: Get right notions and apprehensions of your enemies. We are apt to magnify the creature as if he could do more than he can, and thereby disable ourselves from doing what we should. Possess your souls with the belief of these five things

concerning them: (1.) That they are poor weak enemies (Isa. 40:15, 17, 22), just as a swarm of gnats in the air. See how God describes them in Isaiah 51:13-14; (2.) The little power they have is limited by your God who hath the bounding and ordering of it (John 19:11; Psalm 74:10); (3.) They carry guilt upon them which makes them more timorous than you (Isa. 8:12). Their fear is a strange fear; (4.) They only use carnal weapons against you which cannot touch your souls. If they were praying enemies that could engage God against you, they would be formidable enemies indeed; but this they cannot do. The largest commission that any of them ever had from God extended but to the body and bodily concernment of the saints. They cannot thunder with an arm like God, nor blot your name out of the book of life, nor take your part out of the New Jerusalem—therefore, fear not man; (5.) Your enemies are God's enemies, and God hath espoused your cause and quarrel. The more cruel they are, the kinder he will be to you (John 9:34-35).

5. Rule: Labor to engage the presence of God with you in all places and conditions. Whilst you enjoy this, your spirits will be invincible and undaunted (Josh. 1:9; Psalm 118:6). A weak creature assisted and encouraged by the presence of a great God will be able to do and suffer great things. Poor flesh in the hand of an almighty Spirit acts above itself. A little dog, if his master be by and animates him, will seize upon a beast greater than himself, though he would run from him were his master absent. Our courage ebbs and flows as the manifestations of the divine presence do. Oh, get thyself once within the line of that promise of Isaiah 43:1-2 and thou art invincible.

6. Rule: Get a high estimation of Jesus Christ and all his concernments. They that value him highest, will adventure for

him farthest. Magnanimous Luther, how inestimable a value did he set upon the truths of Christ! *Ruat coelum,* &c. Let heaven rush rather than a crumb of truth should perish. Thou wilt never be a man of zeal and courage for Christ's interest until that interest of Christ hath swallowed up all thine own interests. No sooner is the soul acquainted with and interested in Christ but he heartily blesses all his affairs and concernments. This is that which puts metal and resolution for Christ into the soul.

7. Rule: Beware you be not cheated with maxims of carnal policy that are mistaken for Christian prudence. Many are so, and they prove destructive to all true zeal and courage for Christ. Never was religion professed with greater plainness and simplicity than by the primitive Christians, and never was there a higher spring-tide of courage and zeal for God than in those days. We are apt to call it prodigality and are grown wiser to husband our lives and comforts better than they did. But indeed, our prudentials have even swallowed up our religion. It is true, there is such a thing as Christian prudence, but this doth not teach men to shun all costly and difficult duties and prostitute conscience to save the skin. "A man of understanding walks uprightly" (Prov. 15:21).

8. Rule: Look upon the inside of troubles for Christ as well as upon the outside of them. If you view them by an eye of sense, there appears nothing but matter of discouragement. To look on the outside of a prison, banishment, or death is affrighting and horrible—but if you look into the inside of these things by faith and see what God hath made them to his people, and how joyful and comfortable they have been in these conditions—if you could see what honey they have found in the carcass of a lion, what songs in the stocks and dungeons, what glorying in

tribulation, and hundred-fold reward even in their suffering, then that which looked like a serpent at a distance will appear but as a rod in hand. How many have found themselves quite mistaken in their apprehensions of suffering and have been more loath to come out of a prison than they were to go in! If you did but see your supports and the comforts that souls ordinarily meet with in their troubles for Christ, you would not look on them as such formidable things.

9. Rule: View the issue and reward of suffering by an eye of faith—this also will strongly abate the horror and dread of them (Heb. 10:34). Upon this account, the saints have slighted and contemned them (Rom. 8:18; II Cor. 4:16-17). But then see that you act your faith (1.) Upon the certainty of it—look at it as a most real and substantial thing (Heb. 11:1); (2) View it as a great and glorious reward; and, (3.) View it as near at hand. And then say to thy soul, "Come on my soul, come on; seest thou the joy set before thee, the crown of glory ready to be set on thy head by the hand of a righteous God." Oh, what comparison is there between those sufferings and that glory!

10. Rule: Propound to yourselves the best patterns and examples. Keep your eye upon the cloud of witnesses—these are of special use to beget holy courage (Heb. 12:1; James 5: 10). Who would be afraid to have his name entered on the list of men of whom the world is not worthy and grapple with that enemy that he hath seen so often foiled—and that by a poor weak Christian!? See how the enemy with whom you are to grapple hath been beaten in hand to hand combat and triumphed over by poor women and children! They had as great infirmities, and you have as gracious assistances.

CHAPTER X

The Necessity of a Mortified Heart

Discovering the necessity of a heart mortified to all earthly and temporal enjoyments in order to the right managing of a suffering condition, with several directions for the attaining thereof.

THE next thing wherein your actual readiness for bonds or death consists is in the mortification of your affections to all earthly interests and enjoyments—even the best and sweetest of them. Till this be done, in some measure, you are not fit to be used in any such service for the Lord (II Tim. 1:18). The living world is the very life of temptations. The travailing pains of death are stronger and sharper upon none than those that are full of sense and self. As you see in nature, what conflicts and agonies strong and lively persons suffer when they die—while others, in whom nature is decayed and spent beforehand, die away without half that pain, even as a bird in a shell. Corruption in the saints is like sap in the green wood which resists the fire and will not burn well till it be dried up. Prepared Paul had a heart mortified in a very high degree to all the honor and riches of the world, accounting them all but trifles (Gal 6:14; I Cor. 4:3,4). The need of this will be evinced by these five considerations.

1. Unless the heart be mortified to all earthly enjoyments, they will appear great and glorious things in your eyes and estimation; and if so, judge what a task you will have to deny and leave them all in a suffering hour. It is corruption within that puts the luster and glory upon things without. It is the

carnal eye only that gazes admiringly after them (II Cor. 5:16), and hence the lust is put to express the affection (I John 2:16) because all that inordinate affection we have to them arises from our high estimation of them and that estimation from our lusts that represent them as great and glorious. Therefore, certainly, it will be difficult (if not impossible) to deny them till they have lost their glory in your eye; and that they will never do till those lusts within you that put that beauty and necessity upon them be first crucified. As for instance, what a glory and necessity doth the pride of men put upon the honor and credit of the world so that they will rather choose to die than survive it? But to a mortified soul it is a small matter (I Cor. 4:3). So for riches, how much are they adored till our lusts be mortified? Then they are esteemed but dung and dross (Phil. 3:8). It is our corruptions that paint and gild over these things. When these are crucified, they will be lightly esteemed.

2. Mortification[30] of corruptions is that which recovers a healthful state of soul. Sin is to the soul what a disease is to the body, and mortification is to sin what medicine is to a disease. Hence, those that are but a little mortified are in a comparative sense called carnal (I Cor. 3:3) and babes in respect of weakness. Now, since suffering is some of the Christian's hardest labor and exercise, he cannot be fitted for it until his soul be in an healthful state. A sickly man cannot carry heavy burdens or endure hard labors and exercises. The sick soldier is left behind in his quarters or put into the hospital whilst his fellows are dividing the spoils and

---

[30] The term "mortification" means to put to death—in the context of Christianity, it is the practice of purposefully and prayerfully wrestling with and conquering specific sins (Romans 8:13)—this is the negative side of sanctification. The positive side of sanctification is to prayerfully and purposefully pursue righteousness.

102

obtaining glorious victories in the field. To this sense some expound Romans 8:13, "If ye live after the flesh ye shall die; but if ye, through the Spirit, do mortify the deeds of the body, ye shall live." Just as where mortification is neglected, the soul is in a languishing state and the result of it is death, so where mortification is practiced, the soul is in a healthful and comfortable state and there is life—*vivere pro valere*—so that upon this account also the necessity of mortification of sin appears.

3. Your corruptions must be mortified, else they will be raging and violent in the time of temptation, and like a torrent, they will sweep away all your convictions and resolutions. It is sin unmortified within that makes the heart like gun-powder so that when the sparks of temptation fly about it (and they fall thick in a suffering hour) they do but touch and take. Hence, the corruptions of the world are said to be through lust (II Pet. 1:4). With these internal unmortified lusts the tempter holds correspondence, and these be the traitors that deliver up our souls into his hands.

4. Unless you be diligent and successful in this work, though you should suffer, yet not like a Christian, you will but disgrace religion and the cause for which you suffer—for it is not simply suffering, but suffering as a Christian, that reflects credit on religion and finds acceptance with God. If you be envious, fretful, discontented, and revengeful under your sufferings, what honor will this bring to Christ? Is not this altogether unlike the example of your Lord (Isa. 53:7) and the behavior of suffering saints (I Cor. 4:13)? Thus it will be if your pride, passion, and revenge be not first subdued—for what is the breaking forth of such distempers of spirit but as the flushes of heat in the face from an ill-affected liver? Most

103

certain it is that all the evils are in your natures, and as certain it is, they will rise like mud and filth from the bottom of a lake when some eminent trials shall rake you to the bottom. *Natura vexata prodit seipsam.*

5. Lastly, Mortification must be studied and applied with diligence else you will find many longings and hankerings after earthly enjoyments and comforts which will prove a snare to you. What is sin but the corrupt and vitiated appetite of the creature to things that are earthly and sensual, relishing more sweetness and delight in them than in the blessed God? And what is sanctification but the rectifying of these inordinate affections and placing them on their proper object? A regenerate and mortified Christian tastes not half that sweetness in forbidden fruits that another doth. Set but money before Judas, and see how eagerly he catches at it: "What will ye give me, and I will betray him?" (Matt. 26:15). Set but life, liberty, or any such bait before an unmortified heart and how impotent is he to withstand them as offered in a temptation! Oh, those unmortified lusts! How do they make men hanker, long, and their lips water (as we use to say) after these things? This makes them break prison, decline suffering, though upon the basest terms; whereas a mortified Christian can see all these things set before him, yea, offered to him and refuse them (Heb. 11:35). It is with them much as it was with old Barzillai (II Sam. 19:35). When nature is decayed they find but little pleasure in natural actions (Eccl. 12:1). And look, as the body of sin decays and languishes, so do these longings also. It weans the soul from them all and enables it to live very comfortably without them (Psalm 131; Phil. 4:12). There needs no more to be said to evince the necessity of mortification and discover what influence it hath into a Christian's readiness for sufferings.

104

It remains, therefore, that I open to you some of the principal corruptions about which it mostly concerns you to bestow pains ere suffering comes. There are four principal enjoyments in which you are like to be tried, namely, estate, name, liberty, and life. So the Christian work in suffering times lies in mortifying these four special corruptions. First, the love of the world (estate); secondly, ambition (name); thirdly, inordinate affection of freedom and pleasure (liberty); fourthly, excessive love of life (life).

1. Estate: For the love of this world, away with it, crucify it, crucify it! Down with the idols and let it be dethroned in all that intend to abide with Christ in the hour of temptation. How else will you take the spoiling of your goods? How will you be able to part with all for Christ as these blessed souls did? It grieves my heart to see how many professors of religion are carried captive at the chariot-wheels of a bewitching world. How good would it have been for many professors if they had never tasted so much of the sweetness of this world. Sirs, I beg you for the Lord's sake, down with it in your estimations, down with it in your affections, else temptations will down with you ere long. I shall offer five or six helps for the crucifying of it.

First, Consider your espousals to Christ and how you have chosen and professed him for your Lord and husband. Therefore, your doting upon the world is no less than adultery against Christ (James 4:4). If Christ be your husband, he must be a covering to your eyes; an unchaste glance upon the world wounds him.

Secondly, The more you prize it, the more you will be tormented by it. Did you prize and love it less, it would disquiet and vex you less. It is our dealing on it that makes it draw blood at parting.

105

Thirdly, Get true Scripture-notions of the world and rectify your judgments and affections by them. If you will have the true picture and representation of it drawn by the hand of God himself (see I John 2:16), you will see that it is nothing else but a phantastic glory which passes away. What is become of them that ruffled it out in the world one hundred years ago? What could the world do for them? Are they not all gone down to the sides of the pit? "But he that doth the will of God abideth forever" (I John 2:17).

Fourthly, Study and contemplate Christ and the things above more—this would veil all its glory and kill it at the root (Phil. 3:18-21). Just as a man that hath been gazing upon the sun, when he takes his eyes off that bright and glorious creature and looks to the earth there is a veil of darkness overspreading the face of it that he can see nothing. I wonder how such as pretend to live above and enjoy communion with God can ever relish such sweetness in the world or have their hearts enticed and captivated by it.

Fifthly, Remember always that by your love and delight in worldly things you furnish the devil with the chief bait he hath to catch and destroy your souls. Alas! Were your hearts but dead to these things, he would want a handle to catch hold on. What hath he more to offer you and tempt you from Christ with but a little money or some such poor temporal rewards? And how little would that soul be moved by such a temptation that looks on it all but as dirt?

Sixthly, and lastly, Take notice of the approaches of eternity. Remember you are almost at the end of time, and when you come to launch out into that endless ocean, how will these things look then? It seems glorious whilst you are in the chase and pursuit of it, but upon a deathbed you will see what a deceitful and vain thing it is. Stand by the beds of dying men and hear how they speak of it. O the difference between our

106

apprehensions then and now! Thus, labor to wean off your affections and crucify them to the world.

2. Name: Mortify your ambition and vain affectation of the repute and credit of the world. Oh, stand not on so vain a thing as this. Judge it but a small thing to be judged of man, to have your names cast out as evil. Let not scoffs and reproaches be such terrible things to you. It is, without doubt, a great trial, else the Holy Ghost had not added a peculiar epithet to it which is not given to any other of the sufferings of the saints—not cruel tortures, nor stonings, nor burnings, nor slaying with the sword but "cruel mockings" (Heb. 11:36). Yet learn to be dead to and unaffected by these things; regard the reproaching world as light and low as it regards you. Despise the shame as your master Christ did (Heb. 12:2). And to promote mortification in this, take these helps:

First, Consider this is no new or strange thing that hath happened to you. The holiest of men have past through the same, if not worse, trials (Heb. 10:33; Psalm 44:14). Reproaches have been the lot of the best men. They called Athanasius, Sathanasius; Cyprianus, Coprianus—a gatherer of dung; blessed Paul, a pestilent fellow; Dr. Story threw a faggot at sweet Mr. Denlie's face as he was singing a psalm in the midst of the flames, saying, I have spoiled a good old song.

Second, It may be religion hath been reproached and scoffed at for your sakes; and if so, think it not much to be reproached for religion's sake.

Third, It is much better to be reproached by men for discharging duty than by your own consciences for the neglect of it. If all be quiet within, never be moved at the noise and clamor without. If you have a good roof over your head, be not troubled though the winds and storms bluster abroad (I Pet.

4:14). Take heed what you do, and be heedless what the world says.

Fourth, Always remember that you neither stand nor fall at the world's judgment, and therefore you have less reason to be troubled by it (I Cor. 4:3).

Fifth, There is a worth and excellency in the reproaches of Christ as bad as they seem; and such an excellency as is not to be matched by any earthly enjoyment (Heb. 11:26). The reproaches of Christ are of more worth than the treasures of Egypt, though Egypt then was the magazine of the world for treasures. The apostles counted them their honors (Acts 5:41). When Ludovicus Marsacus, a knight of France, saw those that were to suffer with him in chains, and that they put none upon him because of the nobility of his birth, he said to the executioner, *"Cur me non quoque torqui donast et illustris illius ordinis militem non creas?"* that is, "Why do ye not honor me with a chain, too, and create me a knight of that noble order?"

Lastly, Should scoffs and reproaches scare you from Christ and duty, then, though you should escape the reproaches of men, yet you shall fall under the everlasting contempt of God, angels, and good men. Therefore, "Fear ye not the reproaches of men that shall die, nor be afraid of their revilings, for the moth shall eat them up like a garment, and the worm shall eat them like wool, but my righteousness shall be forever and my salvation from generation to generation," (Isa. 51:7-8).

3. Liberty: Mortify your inordinate affections of liberty, pleasure, and delicate living. O let not a prison seem so formidable to you. It is true, as Christ told Peter in John 21:18, "When thou wast young, thou girdest thyself and walkedst whither thou wouldst; but when thou shalt be old, thou shalt stretch forth thine hands, and another shalt gird thee, and carry

108

thee whither thou wouldst not." You have now your liberty to go whither you will, and it is a precious mercy if well improved. The birds of the air (as one said) had rather be in the woods at liberty, though lean and hungry, than in a golden cage with the richest fare. But yet, if God will call you to deny this also for Christ, see that you be ready to be bound as Paul was and to receive the chain and bonds of Christ with thanksgiving. To which end consider:

First, That the affliction, in such cases of restraint, is more from within than from without you. There is no place but may be delectable to you if your heart be heavenly and the presence of God be engaged with you. What a sweet night had Jacob at Bethel! Paul and Silas in the stocks! See that precious letter of Pomponius *Algerius. Transtulit in coelum Christi proesentia claustrum; Quid faciet coelo? quoe coelum jam creat antro.*[31] It is your own unbelief and impatience that gives you more trouble than the condition.

Second, No prison keeper can keep the Comforter from you if you be the Lord's prisoners (Acts 16). If they could bar out the Spirit from you, it would be a dismal place indeed. But ordinarily, the saints have their clearest visions of God and sweetest presence of the Spirit while in prison. You are the Lord's freemen whilst men's prisoners. All the world cannot divest you of the state of liberty Christ hath purchased for you (John 8:36).

Third, Though a prison looks sad and dismal, yet it is not hell. Oh, bless God for that, though it is a sad prison indeed! Beloved, men have their prisons and God hath his. God's prison is a terrible prison indeed, thousands are now there in chains (I Pet. 3:19), and there you deserve to have already

---

[31] If the presence of Christ once changed a prison into a kind of heaven, what will it do in heaven itself, which even here doth make a dungeon like heaven?

been sent. If God exchanged for you a hell for a prison, have you any cause to complain?

Fourth, How obdurate and cruel whatsoever men are to you, yet the Lord Jesus is kind and tender-hearted to his prisoners. He puts the kindnesses that any show them upon his own account (Matthew 25:40). "He looks, down from heaven to hear the sighs and groans of his prisoners" (Psalm 102:20). He will tenderly sympathize with you in all your prison-straits and troubles.

Fifth, A prison hath been handselled and perfumed by the best and holiest of men in all ages (I Kings 22:27; Jer. 32:2. Matt. 4:12; Acts 5:18; 16:24). God hath made it a settled school of discipline to them.

Sixth, Should you, to avoid a prison, commit a sin instead of being man's prisoner, you shall be clapt up by God, for he hath a prison for your souls even in this world (Psalm 142:7). And this is ten thousand times more dreadful than any dungeon in the world. Oh, it is a dark prison! There is nothing to let in the least beam of God's countenance upon your poor souls. What a sad exchange have you made then.

Seventh, Consider what a ground of comfort God hath laid in that word to obviate the fears and terrors incident to us in such a condition (Rev. 2:10). God hath limited Satan and his instruments, both for time, number, and all circumstances of the trial.

Lastly, You do not know what a mercy may be in it. It may be a time of retirement from the world and the clamors and distractions that are abroad. These days of imprisonment may be your holy days, as a prisoner of Christ once called them.

4. Life: Get a heart mortified to the excessive and inordinate love of life. This, I confess, is the highest and hardest point of

self-denial because it wraps up all other self-interests in it. But yet consider:

First, Though life be very dear, yet Jesus Christ is ten thousand times dearer than thy life. If you be a saint, he is the life of thy life and the length of thy days. In comparison with him and his glory, saints have despised and slighted their lives (Luke 14:26; Rev. 12:11).

Secondly, Die you must, and if by shrinking from Christ you should protract a miserable life for a few days longer, in the mean time you have lost that which is better than life (Psalm 63:3; Matt. 10:39). Oh! When you lie upon your death-bed you will wish that you had obeyed God's call and so have departed in peace.

Thirdly, If you have cordially covenanted with Christ (as all sincere believers have done) then you have yielded up your lives to him to be disposed of for his glory (Rom. 14:7). So that as Christ both lived and died for you, you ought also to live as Christ. And all the excellency you see in life consists in that reference and subservience it hath to his glory. I say then, if you have understandingly and cordially transacted in a covenant-way with him, your care will not be so much how to shun death as by what death you may most glorify God (John 21:19). And certainly you can never lay your life down upon a more honorable and comfortable account than in his cause and for his sake. It was a great trouble to Luther that he carried his blood to his grave.

Fourthly, To die for Christ is one of the highest testifications of your love to Christ that you are capable of (John 13:37). Yea, it is such a testification of your love to the Lord Jesus as angels are not capable of making.

Fifthly, Why should you decline even a violent death for Christ when the bitterness of death shall so soon be past and there is no hell following the pale horse? It cannot separate you from Christ (Rom. 8:38).

Sixthly, Think what a death Christ suffered for you in which the fullness of the wrath of God and man met together so that he was sore amazed; yet "with desire did he desire" it for your sakes (Luke 22:15).

Lastly, Think what a life you shall have with Christ as soon as you are delivered up to and for him (II Tim. 2:12). It is but a wink, and you shall see God. Oh that these things might provoke you to follow on and ply the work of mortification.

CHAPTER XI

The Methods and Mysteries of Satan

Wherein is opened the singular advantage that suffering saints have by their skill and insights into the methods and mysteries of Satan's temptations—some of those wiles of Satan opened and rules for the avoiding of the danger briefly prescribed.

THE hazards and dangers of Christians in times of persecution arise not so much from their suffering as from the temptations that always attend them and are by Satan planted upon their suffering—for the most part, suffering and temptation go together (Heb. 11:37). And therefore, it behooves such as are or expect to be called to suffer to dive into the mysteries of temptation and to be well acquainted with the enemy's designs upon them. So was Paul, and so he supposes all others to be that engage in the same cause. "We are not ignorant of his devices" (II Cor. 2:11). There is a manifold advantage redounding[32] to suffering saints thereby.

1. He that is well acquainted with the methods of temptation will be better able to descry[33] the first approaches and beginnings of it, which is to more than half conquer it. It is a special artifice of Satan to shuffle in his temptations as undiscernibly as possible into the soul, for he knows that "in vain is the net spread in the sight of any bird" (Prov. 1:17). Therefore, he ordinarily makes a suffering season to be a tempting season, because suffering, like fire to iron, makes it

---

[32] to accrue or arise to someone's benefit; having an advantageous effect upon
[33] to discover or perceive something unclear or distant

impressive and operable—they do ordinarily put the soul into a hurry and distraction, and so give him an advantage to tempt the soul with less suspicion and greater success. But now, a skillful Christian that is acquainted with his wiles will discern when he begins to enter into temptation, as Christ's expression is (Luke 22:46). So check the temptation in its first rise when it is weakest and most easily broken. Doubtless one reason why so many fall by temptation is because it has gotten within them and hath prevailed far before it was discovered to be a temptation.

2. He that is well acquainted with Satan's methods of tempting will not only discern it sooner than another, but also knows what his work and duty is and how to manage the conflict with it, which is a great matter. There are many poor souls that labor under strong temptations and know not what to do. They go up and down complaining from Christian to Christian, whilst the judicious Christian plies to the throne of grace with strong cries (II Cor. 12:8), keeps up his watch (Luke 22:46), and countermines the temptation by assaulting that corruption and by endeavors of mortification, which Satan assaults by temptation (I Cor. 9:27).

3. Lastly, To name no more, the one who is best acquainted with the mystery of temptation and can maintain his ground against it, he shall be the persevering Christian under persecutions and the victorious Christian over them. Here lies the main design of Satan in raising persecution against the saints. It is not so much their blood that he thirsts after as their fall. All persecutions are designed by him to introduce his temptations. These work upon our fear, and fear drives us into his trains and snares (Prov. 29:25). The devil's work in raising persecution is but as the fowler's work in beating the bush in

114

the night when the net is spread to take the birds which he can affright out of their hiding places. He that understands that is not easily moved by the strongest opposition from his place and duty, and so is like to prove the most constant and invincible Christian in times of persecution.

Oh then, how necessary it is, since all persecutions are intended as means to promote temptation, to have that skill and insight into these designs of Satan so as to possess advantages to frustrate his designs? I say, how necessary it is that you should be thoroughly instructed wherein the strength of temptation lies, and also, how to resist those strong and dangerous temptations which your sufferings only are intended to usher in.

It will not be unseasonable or impertinent then in this chapter to show you: (1.) Wherein the force and efficacy of temptation lies; and (2.) What you are to do when in a suffering hour such temptation shall assault you. And first,

Question: Wherein doth the efficacy and power of temptation lie?
Answer: It lies principally in three things:

I. In the kind and nature of the temptation
II. In the craft and policy of Satan in managing it
III. In that secret correspondence that Satan hath with our corruptions

I. The power of temptation lies in the kind and nature of the temptation itself, for it is most certain that all temptations are not alike forcible and dangerous. Some are ordinarily more successful than others, and such are these that follow.

1. Strange and unusual temptations—I mean not such as none have been troubled with before us, for there is not a dart in Satan's quiver but hath been shot at the breasts of other saints before it was leveled at ours (I Cor. 10:13). But by strange and unusual, I mean such as the people of God are but rarely troubled with, and possibly were never exercised with before. These are the more dangerous because they daunt and amaze the soul, and ordinarily beget despondency, even as some strange disease would do that we know not what to make of nor can we learn from others who have been sick with it.

2. Mark them for most dangerous temptations that are adapted and suited to your proper sin or evil constitution. For certainly, it is the most dangerous crisis of temptation when it tries a man there. Now, if he be not truly gracious, he falls by the root irrecoverably (Luke 22:5-6). Or if sincere, yet without special assistance and extraordinary vigilance, he falls scandalously (II Sam. 11:2 compared with I Sam. 16:12).

3. When it is a spiritual temptation which rises undiscernibly out of the Christian's duties. This is the less suspected because temptations usually come from the strength and liveliness of corruptions, but this temptation comes from the slaughter and conquests we make of temptations. Duties, and enlargements in them, which are the poison of other lusts, prove the food and fuel of this kind of spiritual pride (I Cor. 4:7-8). And how much the more covert and close any temptation is, the more dangerous it is.

II. The strength and efficacy of temptation lies much in the skill and policy of Satan in the management of it. And hence, they are called wiles, methods, and devices (II Cor. 2:11; Eph. 6:11) and himself an old serpent (Rev. 12:9). And among the rest of his deep and desperate stratagems, these following are remarkable:

1. Satan works by employing such instruments to manage his temptations as are least suspected and have the greatest influence. A Teacher (Gal. 2:14), a wife (Gen 3:6; Job 2:9), friends (Acts 21:13). The devil knows it is a bad business, and therefore he must make the best of it. Paul's sorest trial was by his dearest friends.

2. Satan works by the orderly disposition and ranging of his temptations, beginning with little things first, and then by degrees working over to greater. His first motions are commonly most modest (Gen. 3:1). Should we discover the depth of his design at first, it would startle the soul and make it reply as Hazael, "Am I a dog that I should do thus?" (II Kings 8:13). It is far easier for him to gain his end by increments than by putting forward everything all at once.

3. Satan works by endeavoring to engage the soul upon his own ground. I mean to tempt him from his station and duty where God sets and expects to find him. He knows while you are with God, God is with you (II Chron. 15:2). Whilst a man abides there, he abides with God (I Cor. 7:24). Whilst he is there, the promise is a good breast-work to keep off all his darts. And therefore, as fishermen, when they have spread their nets in the river they beat the fishes out of their coverts and caverns, so doth Satan.

4. Satan works by not presenting the temptation till the soul be prepared to receive it. He loves to strike when the iron is hot. He first lets their troubles come to a height, brings them to the

117

prison, gibbet, or fire, and then offers them deliverance (Heb. 11:35, 37).

5. Satan works by tiring our souls with a long continuance of temptations. What he cannot win by a sudden storm he hopes to gain by a tedious siege. Forty days together he assaulted the Captain of our salvation (Mark 1:13). And truly it is a wonder the soul yields not at last that hath been tried long. "When the rod of the wicked lies long upon the back of the righteous, it is much if he put not forth his hand to iniquity" (Psalm 125:3).

6. Satan works by falling most violently upon them when they are lowest and most prostrate in their spirits and comforts. So he assaulted Job with a temptation to curse God and die when he sat in that deplorable state upon the dunghill (Job 2:8-9). He loves to fall upon us, as Simeon and Levi did upon the Shechemites, when we are sore and wounded. And therefore, ordinarily you find times of divine desertions to be times of diabolical temptations. Just as the wild beasts of the desert come out of their dens in the night and roar after their prey (Psalm 104:20), so doth Satan when the soul seems to be benighted and lost in the darkness of spiritual troubles. And this is the second thing wherein the efficacy and strength of temptation lies.

III. Lastly, temptation lies in that secret correspondence Satan holds with our bosom enemy—our flesh. Were it not for this domestic traitor, he could not surprise us so easily. As you see in Christ, he could do nothing because he found nothing upon which to fasten a temptation. He was like a crystal glass filled with pure fountain water, so that though he should have been agitated and shaken by temptation, yet no filthy sediment could appear; but now we have an enemy within (that is, our flesh) that holds intelligence with Satan, and this would prove a devil to us if there were no other devil to tempt us (Jam. 1:14-15). The flesh is a fountain of temptation in itself (Matthew 15:19) and the chief instrument by which Satan doth all his tempting work (II Pet. 1:4).

Our passions and affections are the handles of his temptations. Everything, said Epictetus, hath δυο λαβασ, *duo labas,* two handles to take it by. Our affections are the handles of our souls. The temptation of self-confidence and pride takes hold of a daring and forward disposition, while the temptation of apostasy upon a timorous disposition. These inbred lusts go over to the enemy in the day of battle and fight against the soul (I Pet. 2:11). This is a more dangerous enemy than the devil. It is true that they both work against us, but with a double difference. Satan works externally and objectively, but lust works internally and physically, i.e., *quoad materale*, as it is capable of physical efficiency. "Sin wrought in me all manner of concupiscence[34]" (Rom. 7:8). Yea, it is a subtle enemy that doth his business politically (Rom. 7:11). Sin deceived me. It betrays with a kiss and strangles with a silken halter. These are his agents, sitting at the council-table in our own breasts and there carrying on his designs effectually. Yea, the flesh is the restless and perpetual enemy—no ridding your bands of him. Satan is sometimes put to flight by resistance (Jam. 4:7) and sometimes ceases his temptations (Luke 4:13). But when he ceases to tempt and inject, this ceases not to irritate and solicit. Wherever we are, temptation will be. It is our sad lot to be tied to it and perpetually assaulted by it (Rom. 7:24). We may say of it as Hannibal said of Marcellus that it is never quiet, whether a conqueror or conquered; yea, it is a potent enemy too—it hauls men away to the commission of

---

[34] i.e., desire

119

sin (Jam. 1:14). It seizes the magazine of the soul and delivers up the arms, I mean the members, to be οπλα αδικιασ, *hopla adikias*, weapons of unrighteousness.

Thus you see wherein the efficacy and power of temptation consists. And it mightily concerns you that are or expect to be sufferers for Christ to be acquainted with these things and to know where the strength of your enemy lies.

But how shall the suffering saint so manage himself in a suffering hour so as not to be defeated by temptations? This brings me upon the second thing I promised, that is, to prescribe some rules for the escaping or conquering of those temptations that are incidental to a suffering state. And first,

1. Rule: Labor to cut off the advantages of temptations before they come. It is our inordinate love to life, estate, liberty, and ease that gives the temptations so much strength upon us. Do not overvalue them, and you will more easily part from them (Rev. 12:11). O mortify self-love and creature-love. Let your heart be loosed and weaned from them, and then the temptation hath lost its strength.

2. Rule: Secure to yourselves an interest in the heavenly glory. Once you clearly see your propriety in the kingdom above, all things on earth will be lower and of less value. Hebrews 10:34 is a pregnant text to this purpose. It is our darkness and uncertainties about those [i.e. eternal things] that make us cling so fast to these [i.e. earthly things].

3. Rule: Settle this principle in your heart as that which you will never depart from—that it is better for you to fall into any suffering than into the least sin (Heb. 11:24-25). All will acknowledge this, but how few practice it! Oh that you would practically understand and receive it! Suffering is but a

respective, external, and temporal evil, but sin is a universal, internal, and everlasting evil.

4. Rule: Believe that God hath cursed and blasted all the ways of sin so that they shall never be a shelter to any soul that flies to them for refuge (Mark 8:35). Proverbs 13:15 says the way of transgressors is a hard and difficult way. There is no security in the way of iniquity. He that runs from suffering to sin, runs from the seeming danger to the real danger, from the painted lion to the living lion.

5. Rule: Live up to this principle that there is no policy like sincerity and godly simplicity. This will preserve and secure you when carnal wisdom will expose and betray you (Psalm 25:2; Job 2:3). Sinful policy never thrives with saints.

6. Rule: Consider sadly what the consequence of yielding yourselves to temptations will be—the name of God will be dreadfully reproached (II Sam. 12:14); a fatal stumbling-block is laid before the blind world (I Sam. 2:27-36); the hearts of many upright ones made sad (Psalm 25:3); the fall of a professor is as when a standard-bearer faints, and "a dreadful wound" it will be to thine own conscience (II Cor. 2:7). One hour's sleep of security may keep you many days and nights waking upon the rack of horror.

7. Rule: Never engage a temptation in your own strength, but go forth against it trembling in yourselves and relying on Divine aids and assistances (Eph. 6:10). What! Are you to grapple with spirits, to enter the lists with principalities and powers? Or what is your strength that you should hope?

8. Rule: Let the days of your temptation be days of strong cries and supplications. Thus did Paul (II Cor. 12:8; Psalm 109:4). Your best posture to wrestle with temptation is upon your knees.

9. Rule: Dwell upon the consideration of those choice encouragements that God hath laid up in the world for such a time. (1.) Though he give Satan leave to tempt you, yet you are still in his hand to preserve you (Deut. 33:3; John 10:28). (2.) That whilst Satan is sifting and trying you on earth, Christ is interceding for you in heaven (Luke 22:31-32). (3.) That an eternal reward is laid up for those that overcome (Luke 22:28-29; Rev. 21:7-8). And now is this reward to be won or lost.

10. Rule: Lastly, be content till God open a door out of your temptations (I Cor. 10:13). The time of the promise will come (Acts 7:17). Wait for it, though it tarry, and seem to be deferred; in the end, it will speak and not lie (Hab. 2:3). There was a secret door in the ark, though it could not be seen whilst the waters prevailed. And so there is in all your temptations, though at present it be not discernible to you.

And thus have I brought you one step nearer to Paul's blessed frame. O give diligence to make yourselves ready for sufferings.

CHAPTER XII

The Necessity of Prayer

Acts 21:13 shows that a choice part of our preparation and readiness for suffering consists in the improvement of our praying abilities and keeping close with God in that heavenly and excellent duty in days of suffering; wherein also is opened the nature and means of its improvement.

PRAYER is said to be amongst duties as faith is amongst the graces. Doubtless it is of special use and service at all times to a Christian. Yet in suffering days, it is of more than ordinary use and necessity (Heb. 4:16; James 5:13). Therefore, it is reckoned among those choice pieces of amour which suffering saints are to put on (Eph. 6:18). I will here briefly discover the necessity of it and then show you that a Christian may improve himself to an excellent degree in it; and lastly, I will prescribe some means for an improvement.

The necessity of it to a suffering saint will demonstratively appear if you consider:

1. That prayer is the outlet of troubles and the best way the poor Christian hath to ease his heart when surcharged with sorrow. Griefs are eased by groans. Such evaporations disburden and cool the heart as the opening of a vein in some cases doth. Oh, the sensible ease that comes in this way! When grief in the mind, like vapors in the air, is condensed into black clouds that overspread the soul and darken that beautiful light that once shone there, then prayer, like the sun, dispels and scatters it (I Sam. 1:18). Many a saint, by prayer, hath sucked the breast of a promise and then fallen asleep by divine

contentment in the bosom of God. A time may come when thy heart is ready to break with trouble and there existeth not a friend to whom thou canst open and ease it, and then blessed be God for prayer (Micah 7:5-7). What sinks others is when troubles fill and overwhelm their hearts and they look to reason, merry company, or outward comforts. But, alas! This is to palliate a cure, and it returns again with the more violence. But prayer gives sensible relief (see the title of Psalm 102; Psalm 62:8). For, (1.) This opens and gives a vent to troubles (Jer. 20:12); (2.) It gives our troubles a diversion and so a cure (Psalm 5:1) and the last verse (v.12) compared; (3.) By praying over them they are not only diverted but sanctified, and so they cease to be distracting or destroying troubles.

2. As prayer gives a vent to our troubles, so it gives an inlet to unspeakable comforts and consolations. See a pregnant instance of this (Acts 16:25). For hereby they obtain gracious answers from the Lord concerning their troubles (II Cor. 12:9). In this also they meet the gracious smiles of God which swallow up their troubles (Psalm 85:8). And, lastly, hereby they prevail with God to open a seasonable and effectual door out of all their troubles (Psalm 34:4-6).

3. Prayer begets and maintains holy courage and magnanimity in evil times. When all things about you tend to discouragement, it is your being with Jesus that makes you bold (Acts 4:18-20). He that is used to coming before a great God will not be afraid to look such little things in the face as most men are. The woman clothed with the sun had the moon under her feet. And what need you have of courage in evil times hath been already shown.

4. Prayer is a duty you may perform at any time or in any condition. No adversary can cut you off from it. It cannot be said so of many other duties. None can hinder the intercourse between heaven and your soul. You may perform it in a prison (Acts 16:25) or in a banished condition (Psalm 61:2). And so you are fitted for a suffering condition.

5. Lastly, You must strive to excel in prayer, forasmuch as no grace within, or service without, can thrive without it. God hath ordained the whole work of grace to grow up to perfection through prayer. He will have all mercies fetched this way (Ezek. 36:37; Jer. 29:11-13). All that comes from God to you, or to you from God, must come in through the channel of prayer. Be convinced then of the need you have to improve yourselves herein, as ever you hope to stand in the evil day.

But how are these praying abilities capable of improvement in the people of God? Praying abilities are either external and common, or internal and special. The external and common ability is nothing else but that dexterity and skill men get to express themselves to God in prayer. Thus, many can put their meaning into apt and decent expressions to which the Spirit sometimes adds his common touches upon the affections. And this hypocrites rest on and glory in. On the contrary, some prayers are special and internal, whereby men are enabled to pour out their souls to God in a gracious manner. And this may be considered either in the habit or the act. The habit is given by the Spirit when the principles of grace are first infused into the soul (Zech. 12:10; Acts 9:11). By being sanctified we are made near, and by acting those principles in prayer we are said to draw near (Psalm 10:17). Now in our actual drawing near to God, the Spirit hath the chief and principal hand. And his assistance therein is threefold.

1. He excites the heart to the duty; it is he that whispers to the soul to draw nigh to God (Psalm 27:8).

2. He suggests the matter of our prayers and furnishes us with the materials (Rom 8:26), guiding us as to the matter, not only to what is lawful, but also to what is expedient for us.

3. He stirs up suitable affections in prayer (Rom. 8:26), hence those groans and tears, those gaspings and vehement anhelation. But notwithstanding all our abilities, both habitual and actual, are from the Spirit and not from ourselves, yet are they capable of improvement by us. For though in respect of acquirement there be a great difference between natural and supernatural habits, yet their improvement is in the same way and manner, and this improvement may be made divers ways.

First, Though you have the Spirit, and can pray, yet you may learn to pray more humbly than before. Though you rise no higher as to words, yet you may learn to lay yourselves lower before the Lord, as Abraham and Ezra did (Gen 18:27; Ezra 9:6).

Secondly, You may learn to pray with more sincerity than formerly. Ah! There is much hypocrisy and formality in our prayers, much of custom. Now you may learn to pour out more cordial prayers (Psalm 17:1; 119:10).

Thirdly, You may learn to pray with more zeal and earnestness than before. Some saints have excelled and been remarkable for this (Dan. 9:19; Hosea 12:4; James 5:16).

Fourthly, Pray with more assiduity and readiness at all times. Ephesians 6:18, "Praying always, with all prayer." Hence, Christ gives that commendation to the church in Song of Solomon 4:11, "Thy lips, O my spouse, drop as the honey-comb." The honey-comb often drops but always hangs full of drops ready to fall.

Fifthly, You may learn to pray with more faith. Oh, the qualms of unbelief that go over our hearts in a duty. Faith is the soul of prayer, and according to the faith that God finds in prayers, he accepts and values it. Now in all these things you may improve yourselves abundantly by:

1. Being more frequent in the duty. Job 22:21, "Acquaint thyself with the Almighty." In the Hebrew it is, "accustom thyself." Those that have been excellent have also been abundant in it (Psalm 5:7).

2. Taking heed that you grieve not the Spirit on whose influences and assistances you so entirely depend, even as much as a ship doth upon the gales of wind for its motion.

3. Honoring the Spirit which enables you to pray, and that especially in two ways: (1.) By dependence on him; go not forth in your own strength to the duty, trust not to your own promptness or preparations; (2.) By returning with thankfulness, ascribing the praise of all to him. Be humble under all enlargements. Say, "Not I, but grace" (I Cor. 15:10).

4. Searching your own hearts and examining your necessities and wants when you draw nigh to God. This will be a fountain of matter and will give you a deep resentment[35] of the worth of mercies prayed for.

---

[35] The archaic use of this word meant "strong perception of good."

127

5. Lastly, by looking more at the exercise of graces and less at the discovery of parts; by laboring for impressions more and pumping for expressions less. And thus I have briefly shown you how to furnish yourselves with this needful qualification also.

CHAPTER XIII

The Necessity of Dependence Upon Christ

In this chapter is shown the necessity of going out of ourselves, even when our habitual and actual preparations are at the greatest height, and depending as constantly and entirely upon the Spirit, who is Lord of all gracious influences, as if we had done nothing, together with the means of working the heart to such a frame.

THUS you have seen your habitual and actual readiness for suffering, and blessed is the soul that gives diligence to this work. But now, lest all that I have said and you have wrought should be in vain, I must let you know that all this will not secure you unless you can, by humility, faith, and self-denial, go out of yourselves to Christ and live upon him daily for supply of grace, as much as if you had none of all this furniture and provision for suffering. I confess grace is a very beautiful and lovely creature, and it is hard for a man to look upon his own graces and not dote upon them. But yet know, that if you had all these excellent preparations that have been mentioned, yea, and all angelical perfections superadded, yet are you not complete without dependence upon Christ (Col. 2:10). Whenever you go forth to suffer for Christ, you should say at the head of all your excellent graces, duties, and preparations as Jehoshaphat did when at the head of a puissant and mighty army in II Chron. 20:12, "O Lord, I have no might nor strength, but my eyes are unto thee." This is one thing in which Paul excelled and was a special part of his readiness (I Cor. 15:10). What a poor creature is the most imminent saint left to himself in an hour of trial? The hop, the ivy, and the woodbine are taught by nature to cling about stronger props and supporters. What they do by nature, we should do by grace. The necessity and great advantage of this will appear upon diver considerations.

1. Consideration: Consider the Christian's own imbecility[36] and insufficiency, even in the strength and height of all his acquirements and preparations. What are you to grapple with such an adversary? Certainly you are no match for him that conquered Adam hand to hand in his state of integrity. It is not your inherent strength that enables you to stand but what you receive and daily derive from Jesus Christ. John 15:5, "Without me," or never so little separated from me, "ye can do nothing." All your sufficiency is of God (II Cor. 3:5). Upon this very consideration the apostle exhorted the Ephesians "to be strong in the Lord, and in the power of his might," i.e., not to depend upon their own stock and furniture but upon divine assistances and daily communications. "For we wrestle not with flesh and blood but principalities and powers" (Eph. 6:10-12). In his own strength shall no man prevail.

2. Consideration: It is the great design of God in the gospel to exalt his Son and to have all glory attributed and ascribed to him, "that in all things he might have the pre-eminence" (Col. 1:18) that Christ "might be all in all" (Col. 3:11). Hence, no saint may have a self-sufficiency or be trusted with a stock as Adam was, but Christ being filled with all the fullness of God and made the πρωτον δεκλικον, *proton deklikon*, or first receptacle of all grace. "For it pleased the Father that in him all fullness should dwell." All the saints are therefore to go to him for supplies and of his fullness to receive (John 1:16).

---

[36] i.e., want of strength

This fullness being a ministerial fullness, like that of the sun or of a fountain, is intended to supply all our wants. And hence, it is that faith, which is a self-emptying and self-denying grace, that is appointed to be the instrument of fetching our supplies from Christ. All must be derived from him that all the praise and glory may be ascribed to him (Phil. 4:19). And this is a most wise and congruous ordination of God, for hereby not only are his people better secured, but by this also the reproach that lay upon Christ is rolled away. He was reproached on earth as barren, empty, weak. "Can any good come out of Nazareth?" (John 1:46). He was looked upon as a "root springing out of a dry ground" (Isa. 53:2), but by this shall his reproach be wiped away. So unless you will go about to cross the great design of God in the exaltation of his Christ, you must go out of yourselves and humbly and constantly rely upon supplies from Christ and his grace to help in the times of need.

3. Consideration: A Christian is constantly to depend upon Christ, notwithstanding all his own preparations and inherent qualifications, because the activity even of inherent grace depends upon him. Inherent grace is beholden to exciting and assisting grace for all it is enabled to do. You cannot act a grace without his Spirit (I Cor. 15:10; II Cor. 3:5; John 15:5). It may be said of grace in us, as it was of the land of Canaan, "It is not as the land of Egypt, whence ye came out, where thou sowedst thy seed and wateredst it with thy foot as a garden of herbs; but a land of hills and valleys, drinking water of the rain of heaven; a land which the Lord thy God careth for. His eyes are always upon it, from the beginning of the year even to the end of the year" (Deut. 11:10-12). As the life and fragrance of vegetables depends upon the influences of heaven, so do our graces upon Christ. And hence he is called,

131

(1.) a root (Isa. 11:10); (2.) a head (Col. 1:18); (3.) a sun (Mal. 4:2); and (4.) a fountain (Zech. 13:1). All which comparisons do fully carry this truth in them.

4. Consideration: Lastly, in living a life of dependence upon Christ your security lies. Indeed, this is the great difference between the two covenants. In the first covenant, Adam's stock was in his own hands, and so his security or misery depended upon the unconstrained choice of his own mutable and self-determining will. But now in the new covenant, all are to go to Christ to depend upon him for supplies and are thus secured against all destructive dangers (Jude 1; I Pet. 1:5). Should you go forth in your own strength against a temptation, either your grace would fail and you fall in the conflict, or if you obtain any victory over it by your own strength, yet it is a thousand to one but your pride would conquer you when you had conquered it. It would be like him that slew an elephant but was himself slain by the fall of that elephant which he slew. But now, by this way, as God hath secured you against the dangers without, so also the frame and constitution of this new covenant is such as prevents the danger arising from our own pride too. It is not *Ego et Deus mens*, "I and my God did this," as was once said by a profane mouth, but self is abased and the Lord lifted up in his own strength (I Cor. 5:7). And thus, I have briefly evinced the necessity of this daily dependence.

But next it concerns you to know what this dependence we speak of is. This also I shall briefly open to you, laying down somewhat negatively and somewhat positively about it.

1. Negatively: It is not to deny the grace wrought in us by the Spirit. This would be both injustice and ingratitude. We may

know our own graces so as to be thankful for them, though not so as to be proud of them (I Cor. 15:10).

2. Negatively: It is not a lazy excuse from our duty. You do not depend upon but dishonor Christ by your laziness. You must not say that because Christ must do all, therefore I must do nothing; but rather, work out your salvation, because it is he that works both to will and to do (Phil. 2:12, 13). These are not opposed but subordinated.

But then positively, it lies in three things:

1. Positively: In seeing and acknowledging the infinite sufficiency and fullness that is in Christ—to acknowledge him to be all in all, not only by way of impetration procuring all (Heb. 9:12), but also by way of application, bringing home to the soul all the blessings purchased by his blood and settling us in the possession of it (John 14:3). And so from first to last to eye him as the author and finisher of our faith.

2. Positively: In seeing the necessary dependence that all our graces have upon him. So that as you see the stream depending on the fountain, the beam upon the sun, the branch upon the root, the building upon the foundation, even so do our graces upon Christ. On him they live, and if cut off from him, they die. "Our life is hid with Christ in God" (Col. 3:3). When you see this, and also see that all your activity and striving is but as the hoisting up of the sails in order to the motion of the ship which can do nothing till there come a gale, and when you look upon your grace as a creature that must be upheld, fed, acted, and preserved by Christ (Col. 2:9-10,19), then you are prepared for this act of dependence. As for instance, you can never depend upon Christ for the acting of that grace of hope until you see Christ to be the prop and foundation of it—and it

depends upon him as upon its cause (I Pet. 1:3), as upon its object (Heb. 6:19), and as upon its foundation and ground work (Col. 1:27).

You can never depend upon Christ for your joy and comfort until you see what a necessary dependence this also hath upon him (Phil. 3:3) and that both as to its being and acting (John 16:22).

You can never depend upon him for strength in any duty until you see how your duties depend upon Christ, not only for the strength by which they are performed (John 15:4-5) but also for acceptation when they are performed (I Pet. 2:5). It were easy to instance in any other grace.

3. Positively: It lies in looking off from your own grace whenever you are put upon the acting of it (I mean in regard of any dependence upon it) and looking by an eye of faith for acceptation to Christ (Heb. 12:2). To the putting forth of which act of dependence upon Christ, holy ejaculations in our own on-sets upon duty, or those quick and vigorous liftings up of our souls to God that way are of special use, it being a duty fitted for the purpose when there is no room for set and solemn prayer. And to urge you to this duty, I shall offer these seven considerations, which, oh, that they might prevail upon your hearts and make you forever to clasp and cling about Christ more than ever you have done.

1. Consideration: You have little reason to rely upon the strength of your own graces for you may be easily deceived in that matter and think you have much more grace than you have. How often are the common gifts of the Spirit mistaken for his special graces! The sixth chapter to the Hebrews is able to make a man tremble in this thing.

134

2. Consideration: Suppose you have much grace—however, do you not have strong corruptions, and may you not meet with strong temptations also? He that hath less of other graces than you may have more humility and self-denial than you, and so may stand when you fall. Great enlargements are often attended with great temptations of pride.

3. Consideration: Whatever measures of grace you have arrived at, yet all is not able to secure you from falling if God withhold or withdraw his aids and influences. Abraham had more faith than you, and yet he fell into a sin contrary to that very grace wherein he so excelled others (Gen. 20:2). Job had more patience than you. Which of you could behave yourselves as he did had you been in the like circumstances as he was? (Job 1:20-21). He is renowned for it in the Scripture (James 5:11), yet he fell into that sin which is contrary to this grace also (Job 3). Moses had more meekness than you. "Now the man Moses was the meekest man upon the earth" (Num. 12:3). If you be but reproved, and that justly for your faults, how waspish[37] are you? Yet see how this grace failed even in him in an eminent trial of it (Num. 11:13-15). Adam was much more advantaged in this respect than you, being made upright and no corruption inherent in him, yet he fell. The angels more righteous even still, yet they fell. Oh, when will you learn the vanity of self-dependence!?

4. Consideration: Nothing more provokes the Lord to withdraw his Spirit and let you fall than this sin of self-confidence (Luke 14:29-31). God will teach you by sad experience your own weakness and what frail and vain things you be if you will learn it by no other means.

---

[37] i.e., testy, snappish, ill-tempered, resentful

135

5. Consideration: If God permit you to fall (as doubtless he will, if you be self-conceited) then the more eminent you have been or are for grace, the more will the name of God be reproached by your fall. This will furnish the triumphs of the uncircumcised and the lamentations of your brethren and make them say, "How are the mighty fallen!" (II Sam. 1:27). What dismal consequents will attend your fall.

6. Consideration: Have you not sad experience of your own weakness from day to day in your lesser trials? Have you not said in some smaller conflicts, as David once did, "My feet had well nigh slipped" (Psalm 73:2)? O me-thinks this should teach you to look more to God and less to self. "If you have run with footmen, and they have wearied you in the land of peace, think sadly how you should contend with horses in the swellings of Jordan" (Jer. 12:5). Do you not see that you are but feathers in the wind of temptation? Consult your former experiences, and they will tell you what weaklings you are.

7. Consideration: Lastly, hath Christ given you more grace than others? Then how much more hath he obliged you to honor him thereby? And is this your requital of his love!? What! To take the crown from his head and put it upon your own? Certainly a greater injury cannot be done to Christ than this.

Well then, by all this be persuaded to cease from yourselves, yea, from your religious selves; and to all your other preparations, add dependence upon Christ as a choice one. If you do these things, you shall never fall. And thus you see the complete Christian in his equipage for sufferings.

1. The politic and hypocritical professors, whose hearts were never set right at first and therefore cannot be steadfast when trials come (Psalm 78:8). Their hearts were never sound in God's statutes, and therefore, no wonder if they be not only a shame to but ashamed of their profession (Psalm 119:80). Never wonder if you see that profession which began in hypocrisy end in apostasy. These lack their habitual readiness for sufferings and so cannot drink of that cup. As a result, they fall when tried; and when they fall, they fall dreadfully, and often irrecoverably, for they neither have the seed of God in them nor any promise of God made to them. And are there not many such to be found in every place? For, first, how difficult is it to persuade many of you to any duty that hath loss or hazard attending on it? Doth not the sincere heart stand inclinable and disposed to all the known will of God (Psalm 119:6)? Do Christians normally enquire about what is cheap, easy, and safe for them, or what is their duty (Gal. 1:16)? Speak conscience, for to thee do I appeal. Art thou not conscious of some reserves, limitations, and exceptions? Doth not the man, like Naaman, desire the Lord to excuse and pardon him in this or that thing (II Kings 5:17)? And do you think that this is consistent with sincere obedience which accepts duty and does not quarrel with any command because they all flow equally from the sovereignty of God (Jam. 2:11)? So it does what it does *intuitu voluntatus*, that is, upon the sight of God's will. Say conscience, are there not great strugglings, disputes, and contests between thee and fleshly interests in such cases? And art thou not frequently over-borne? Search your hearts in this particular.

Yea, second, I appeal to you whether there be not many among you that choose sin rather than affliction? This is always the hypocrite's option and choice. He judges sufferings the greatest evils and so orders himself in his election. It was

138

merely to avoid persecution that those hypocrites (Gal. 6:12) constrained others to be circumcised only to gratify the Jews. So by a sinful compliance with them, the offense of the cross might cease. If Paul would have done so, he might have avoided it too, but he durst not, whatever the consequences be (Gal. 5:11). O this is a shrewd sign of a false heart. "Be careful, do not turn to evil; for you have preferred this to affliction" (Job 36:21). And the contrary disposition is always found in the upright heart (Heb. 11:25).

Nay, are there not some that have thrown up their professions, and others that are ready to when they see into what difficulties it involves them? Whilst they could live upon the profession of truth, they entertained it, but when truth comes to live upon them, they thrust it out and cry, "Away with this profession, it will beggar[39] and undo us." Then they recant their profession of faith and secretly wish they had never made it in the first place. O examine whether your hearts be not thus turned back and your steps declined. If so, it is manifest you are hypocritical professors and that it was some outward self-respect at first which engaged you in your profession of religion—but this can never enable you to hold out when difficult days come. I say, it is manifest by this departure from your profession that some outward self-respect at first allured you to it. As now, when I behold the artificial motions of the wheels in a watch and see how regularly the needle marks the journal-hours of the sun upon the flat of the quadrant, and see nothing that moves or guides it, it would cause admiration if I had never seen it before or did not understand the cause and motion. But when I look upon the other side and there find wheels, ressorts, counterpoises, and a spring that causes all those motions, I cease to wonder.

---

[39] destroy

Certainly some lust or other was the spring of all thy religious motions. Stop or take off that and motion ceases. And if it be so, this scab of hypocrisy will at last break out into that botch of apostasy. Thou canst never hold out long under trials (Matt. 13:21). Oh, how many such sad sights may we live to see as trials come! Difficult times are coming (II Tim. 3:1). And woe to such then as want sincerity at the bottom of their profession.

2. And as these have no habitual readiness for suffering, and consequently, must be ruined by them, so there are others that may be truly godly and have the root of the matter in them who are yet far from actual readiness; and so continuing, they are likely to be a reproach to religion when their trial comes, for it is not a little grace in the sleepy habit that will secure you from falling scandalously by the hand of temptation. Although that seed of God which is in you will recover you again and prevent total and final apostasy, yet consider what a sad thing it is to enter into and be conquered by temptation—to be led away in triumph by the tempter and made a reproach to Christ. Oh, it is a sad consideration to think how many there be amongst the people of God that discover little or no actual preparations for suffering. As first,

(1.) Upon how many of the saints is the spirit of slumber poured out? Even the wise, as well as foolish, seem now to be asleep. There is a twofold spiritual sleep—the first is total upon wicked men, and it is one of God's sorest and most dreadful strokes upon their souls (Isa. 29:10). The Hebrew word in this verse is the same as that which is used of Adam when God cast him into that deep sleep whilst he took out his rib. And in II Tim. 2:26 it signifies such a sleep as that which is occasioned by drunkenness—out of such a sleep doth the Lord awaken all that are saved, and they never fall into it any

140

more. The other is partial, Song of Solomon 5:2, and is incident to the people of God (Matt. 25:5). This is nothing else but the torpor or sluggishness of spirit which seizes upon the saints; and never did it prevail, I fear, among them more than now. For where is their activity for God? Where is he that stirreth up himself to take hold of God (Isa. 64:7)? Where is there such a generation as that (Psalm 24:6)? We pray, confer, and hear for the most part but as men who speak between sleeping and waking. Where can you find, except here and there, a man that hath a quick and lively sense of God's indignation upon him or who trembles at his judgments? Is not that the very case of the most which God describes (Isa. 42)?

(2.) How many are seized by a private and worldly spirit? Every man is turning to his own house and eagerly pursuing the world. Oh! How are we entangled in the wilderness? How doth the world eat up our time and eat out our zeal? How doth it cowardize and soften our spirits, and render us utterly unfit for the yoke and burden of Christ? You that see so much beauty and taste so much sweetness in the creature will have a hard time when called to deny it. You are not yet prepared to drink of the cup or take up the cross of Christ.

(3.) How many poor Christians are of a low and timorous spirit, ready to tremble at the shaking of a leaf? Ah poor hearts! How unfit are you for bonds or death! This passion of fear that so predominates you is the very passion which Satan assaults and lays siege to in the hour of temptation, as was before noted. And commonly it is occasioned (where it flows not from the natural constitution) from an excessive love to the world or some guilt upon the spirit. It is true, the Lord can assist weak faith and subdue strong fears as that you may be enabled to stand the shock when it comes. For as I noted formerly, our strength lies not in anything inherent in us, but we are strong or weak according to the divine presence and assistances that we enjoy; yet if you labor not to mortify this evil and do not stir up yourselves in the use of all appointed means to rouse your zeal and courage for God, I know no warrant you have to expect such assistances.

(4.) Lastly, how many poor Christians among us are to this day dark and cloudy in their evidences for heaven? Had they walked closely with God, being laborious in the disquisition and search of their own hearts, they had long since obtained a clearness and satisfaction about the state of their own hearts. But as the case stands with them, how unfit are they for bonds or death. Oh! It is a sad case when inward and outward troubles meet together, as you may see in Gen. 42:21-22, when there shall be fightings without and fears within. When such a pang as that in Lamentations 3:17-18, "And my soul has been rejected from peace; I have forgotten happiness. So I say, 'My strength has perished, and so has my hope from the Lord.' " When this pang shall come over thy heart, what wilt thou do?

By all that hath been said, it appears that most professors of the faith are in a very unready posture for suffering, so that when troubles come to a height, we are likely to see many sad spectacles. Many offenses will come. Religion is likely to be wounded in the house of its friends. Oh! What a day of mercy have we enjoyed! What helps and choice advantages, above any precedent age, and yet so unready. How sad and inexcusable is this?

142

CHAPTER XV

The Necessity of Preparing for Greater Trials

Containing another use of the point, by way of exhortation, persuading all the people of God whilst the Lord respites and graciously delays their trials to answer the end of God therein and prepare themselves for greater trials; where several motives are propounded to excite to the duty

UP then from your beds of sloth, awake from your security, O ye saints, get upon your watch-towers, tremble in yourselves, that ye may rest in the day of evil (Hab. 2:1-3). "Put on the whole amour of God, that ye may be able to stand in the evil day, and when you have done all, to stand" (Eph. 6:11). O let it never be said of your dwellings, as it is said of the tabernacles of the wicked in Job 21:9, "Their houses are safe from fear."

Augustus heard of a man that was deeply in debt yet who slept heartily. So he sent for this man's pillow, supposing there was some strange virtue in the pillow! I wonder what pillow ye have gotten, O ye drowsy saints, that you can sleep so quietly upon it now that all things about you are conspiring trouble and threatening danger. Can you sleep like Jonah when seas of wrath are tumbling and roaring round about you and threaten to entomb you and all your enjoyments? Behold, "The stork in the heavens knows her appointed time" (Jer. 8:7) and hath not God made you wiser than the fowls of the air (Job 35:11)? It may be the sound of some present judgment that startles you like a sudden clap of thunder in the air; but how soon doth sloth and security prevail and overcome you again.

They say poison by being habituated may be made innocent.[40] We are so used to, or rather hardened, under calamities that nothing moves or effectually awakens us. Lord, what will the end of these things be? Wilt thou surprise thy people unawares? Shall thy judgments find them secure and leave them desperate? O that God would persuade you "to gather yourselves together, yea, to gather together" (not in an unlawful and seditious way, but in the way of duty) "before the decree bring forth, and the day pass as the chaff" (Zeph. 2:1-2). O prepare to meet your God (Amos 4:12)! Prepare your faith, love, and courage before God calls you to the exercise of them.

And to excite you to this duty, besides all the aforementioned benefits of a prepared spirit, consider these following particulars by way of motive.

1. Motive: Consider the many calls which God hath given you to this work. The Lord hath uttered his voice and called from heaven unto you. Will you be deaf to his calls? He hath called upon you (1.) By the word—God would have it cry to you first because he would give the first honor to his word. He hath given all his prophets one mouth (Luke 1:70) and they have warned you faithfully; (2.) By the rod—this also hath a loud voice (Mic. 6:9; Psalm 2:5). Men of understanding will hear this voice, and those that will not hear it shall be lashed by it even till they are sick with smiting (Psalm 2:13); (3.) By prodigious and portentous signs in the heavens and earth, such as no age can parallel—these have a loud voice to all that regard the works of the Lord or the operations of his hands. Eusebius calls them God's sermons to the world; (4.) O that we were wise to consider what God's ends are in these things!

---

[40] i.e., ineffective, harmless

One observes, "That as they are the plainest and most obvious to sense, so they are commonly the last sermons which God intends to preach to nations before he inflicts his punishment on them if they repent not." O let not God, speaking in ordinary and extraordinary ways to you, still speak in vain. Your preparation for suffering is the most probable means of preventing your fall and ruin by suffering.

2. Motive: Suffering proves fatal and destructive to some but only to secure and careless ones. Such as are diligent and faithful in the use of God's means are secured from the danger. Christ lays our constancy and perseverance very much upon our forecasting the worst that may fall out (Luke 14:28). "Put on the whole amour of God that ye may be able to stand" (Eph. 6:12). He that hath first severed Christ in his thoughts from all worldly advantages and puts the case thus to his own soul, "O my soul, canst thou embrace or love a naked Christ? Canst thou be content to be impoverished, imprisoned, and suffer the loss of all for him?" This is the one who is most likely to cleave faithfully to him when the case is really presented to him indeed. And can it seem a light thing in your eyes to be enabled to stand in such an evil day? If you fall away from Christ, then all you have wrought is lost (Ezek. 33:13). Gideon's one bastard son destroyed all his seventy sons. This act renders all former actions and professions of faith vain. If you fall, you shall thereby be brought into a more perfect bondage to the devil than ever (Matt. 12:45). Yea, ordinarily apostates are judicially given up to be persecutors (I Tim. 1:20) and are seldom or never recovered again by grace (Heb. 6:4, 6). They that lick up their vomit, seldom cast it up anymore. It is a fall within a little as low as the unpardonable sin whence never any rise again. In some cases, the judge will not allow the offender his book. And is it not then a choice and

desirable mercy to escape and prevent such a fall as this? O good souls, ply your preparation-work close then—prepare or perish.

3. Motive: Preparation for suffering will best answer the grace of God in affording you such choice helps and advantages as you have enjoyed. How long have you enjoyed the free liberty of the gospel shining in its luster among you? This sun, which to some other nations hath not risen and to those on whom it hath shined yet it is but as a winter's sun, remote and its beams but feeble, but on you who have lived, as it were, under the line, it hath been over your heads and shed its richest influences upon you. Yea, God's ministers who are not only appointed to be watchmen (Ezek. 3:16-17) but trumpeters to discover danger (Num. 10:8). These have faithfully warned you of a day of trouble and have given you their best assistance to make you ready for it. And is not their joy, yea life, bound up in your stability in such a day of trial? Doth not every one of them call upon you in the words of Philippians 4:1, "Therefore, my brethren, dearly beloved, and longed for, my joy and crown, so stand fast in the Lord, my dearly beloved"? Will it not cut them to the very heart if after all their spending labors among you they still leave you unready as enemies to the cross of Christ, impossible to be reconciled and persuaded to suffering-work for Christ?

I remember I have read of the Athenian Codrus, who being informed by the oracle that the people whose king should be slain in battle should be conquerors, he thereupon disrobed himself, and in a disguise, went into the enemies quarters that he might steal a death to make his people victorious.

Oh! How glad would your ministers be if you might conquer and overcome in the day of temptation whatever became of their lives and liberties! Yea, and if they be offered

146

upon the sacrifice and service of your faith, they can rejoice and joy with you all. Such is their zeal and longing after your security and welfare. But if still you remain an unready people and do become a prey to temptation, oh how inexcusable will you be!

4. Motive: Remember how ready the Lord Jesus was to suffer the hardest and vilest things for you. He had a bitter cup put into his hands to drink for you into which the wrath both of God and man was squeezed. Never had man such sufferings to undergo as Christ. *Dotor Christi fuit major omnibus doloribus*, Aquin. Whether you consider: (1.) The dignity of his person, who was in the form of God and might have stood upon his peerage and equality with him—he who is the sparkling diamond of heaven (Acts 7:56), the darling of the Father's soul (Isa. 42:1), glorious as the only begotten of the Father (John 1:14), yea, glory itself (Jam. 2:1), yea, the very brightness of glory (Heb. 1:3). He is the *delicice Christiani orbis*, fairer than the sons of men. And for him to be so debased below so many thousands of his own creatures, to become a worm and no man—this was a wonderful humiliation. It was Jeremiah's lamentation that such as were brought up in scarlet embraced dunghills, and that princes were hanged up by the hands, and the faces of elders were not reverenced. But what was that to the humiliation of the Lord of glory? Or, (2.) That he suffered in the prime and flower of his years when full of life and sense and more capable of exquisite sense of pain than others, for he was *optima complexionatus* (in the words of Aquinas) of a singular constitution; and all the while he hung on the tree his sense of pain not at all blunted or decayed (Mark 15:37, 39). Or, (3.) The manner of his death. It was the death of the cross, which was a rack to Christ, for in reference to the distention of his

members upon the cross is that spoken in Psalm 22:17, "I may tell all my bones." Or, (4.) That all this while God hid his face from him. When Stephen suffered, he saw the heavens opened. The martyrs were many of them ravished and transported with ecstasies of joy in their sufferings, but Christ was in the dark. He suffered in his soul as well as in his body, and the sufferings of his soul were the very soul of his sufferings. It was the Father's wrath that lay so heavy on him as to put him into such an agony that an instance was never given of the like nature—for he sweat θρομβοι, *thromboi*, great drops or clodders of blood which fell from his body to the ground (Luke 22:44). "It amazed him, and made him very heavy" (Mark 14:33) yea, sorrowful even to "death" (Matt. 26:38).

And yet, as bitter as the cup was, he freely and willingly drank it up (John 18:11) and prepared himself to be offered up a sacrifice (Psalm 40:6-7). "He gave his back to the smiters" (Isa. 50:6) yea, longed exceedingly for the time till it came, (Luke 12:50).

Now, if Christ so cheerfully prepared and addressed himself to such sufferings as these for you, should you not prepare yourselves to encounter any difficulty or hardships for him? O my brethren, doth not this seem a just and fair inference to you from the sufferings of Christ for you? "Forasmuch then as Christ hath suffered for us in the flesh, arm yourselves likewise with the same mind" (I Peter 4:1).

Oh, trifle no longer, feed not yourselves with fancies and groundless presumptions of immunity and peace, but foresee difficulties and fit yourselves to bear them.

CHAPTER XVI

Words of Comfort for Trembling Hearts

Containing the last use of the point by way of support and comfort to poor trembling souls who do take pains to make themselves ready for suffering but yet finding such strength in Satan's temptations and their own corruptions fear that all their labor is vain and that they shall faint and utterly apostatize when their troubles and trials come to an height.

IN the last place, if it be such a blessed thing to be ready for bonds or death for Christ, this may minister much comfort to such souls who though they cannot say as Paul here did (Acts 21:13) that they are ready, yet they are at work daily upon their own hearts to make them ready and strive in the use of all means to conquer those corruptions that hinder it and improve those graces in which it mainly consists. O poor soul, whatever present unreadiness or indisposition thou findest and complainest of in thine heart, yet thy condition is safe.

Objection 1: Oh! But I cannot be satisfied in that. I fear I shall be over-borne by temptations when they come to a height. I have such experience of the deceits and treacherousness of my own heart that it seems impossible to me to do as these blessed souls did when I come to the like trials.

Solution 1: It is well thou suspectest thine own heart and tremblest in thyself; this fear will keep thee waking while others are securely sleeping. It was a good saying of a reverend minister (Mr. A. H.) now with God, "He that fears to

149

flinch shall never flinch for fear." It is true, seeming grace may be totally lost (Luke 7:18; Heb. 6:4-5; II Pet. 2:20). It is granted also that the sin of believers deserves that God should forsake them and that he may suffer grace in them to be sadly abated and they may fall before a temptation as Peter and all the disciples did—but that thou shall never be separated from Christ or fall *totus a toto*, in totum, utterly away from God, thou mayest be abundantly satisfied upon these five grounds.

1. From God's eternal electing love, wherewithal gracious souls are beloved and embraced, be their graces ever so weak or their corruptions ever so strong. This is immutable (Heb. 6:18) and hence it is said in Mark 13:22, "They shall deceive (if it were possible) the very elect." Now, this immutable purpose of God is not founded upon any mutable ground or reason in thee (Rom. 9:11). Yea, when he (Rom. 8:29) elected thee, he saw what thou wouldst be and yet that hindered him not.

2. From the covenant of grace in the bosom of which thou art wrapped up, this is all thy salvation and all thy hope. It will afford thee abundant satisfaction if thou dost but weigh particularly these three things about it: (1.) That the Author of this covenant is not a fickle creature but a faithful God with whom there is not yea and nay; with whom there is no variableness, nor shadow of turning; whose gifts and callings are without repentance; so that once one is within this blessed covenant, one is in it for ever; (2.) That God hath established the covenant with you in the blood of Christ—therefore, the sacramental cup is called "the cup of the New Testament in his blood" (Luke 22:20). The everlasting merit and efficacy whereof gives the soul of a believer the highest satisfaction imaginable. Lastly, add to this that what is in this covenant

150

God hath undertaken for us, as well as for himself, so that what is a condition in one Scripture is the matter of a promise in another (Jer. 32:40).

3. Remember and draw comfort from that strict and intimate union that is between Christ and thee. And hence it is impossible thou shouldst be lost. For: (a.) Thy union with his person brings interest in his properties along with it. Whatever he is, or hath, it is for thee. His eye of knowledge, arm of power, and bowels of pity are all for thee; (b.) This union with his person secures thy feeble graces from perishing (John 4:14). Thy graces have an everlasting spring. Whilst there is sap in this root, it will ascend into the branches; (c.) It implies thy perseverance because by this union thou becomest an integral part of Christ's body, which would be mutilated and defective should thou be cut off and lost; (d.) Thou shalt not be lost because of the prevalent intercession of Jesus Christ in the heavens for all his saints in all their trials here on earth. From hence the apostle infers the certainty of our perseverance (Rom. 8:34) and a pregnant instance of it you have in Peter's case (Luke 22:32). So Hebrews 7:25 speaks fully to the case. To strengthen this, consider: (i.) Who it is that intercedes—it is Christ, whose person is most dear and ingratiated with the Father (John 11:42); (ii.) What he intercedes for—surely for nothing but what is most suitable to his Father's will. The will of Christ and his Father do not clash (John 16:26-27). Yea, what he prays for, he prays not for gratis or asks upon any dishonorable terms to the justice of his Father, but his prayers on your behalf are all mercies purchased and paid for, and therefore fear not the failing of your graces.

4. Your salvation is secure because the Spirit of Christ which dwells and abides in thee and hath begun his saving work

151

upon thee. I say saving for else it would afford no argument. His common works on hypocrites come to nothing, but in thee they cannot fail. For: (a.) His honor is pledged and engaged to perfect it. That reproach of the foolish builder shall never lie upon him that he began to build but could not finish. Besides, this would make void all that the Father and the Son have done for thee; both their works are complete and perfect in their kinds, and the Spirit is the last efficient in order of working; (b.) Besides, the grace he hath already wrought in thee may give thee yet further and fuller assurance of its preservation, inasmuch as it hath the nature of a seal, pledge, and earnest of the whole (Rom. 8:23; II Cor. 1:22). So that it cannot fail.

5. Your salvation is secure based on those multitudes of assertory, promissory, and comparative Scriptures, the rich veins whereof run through the book of God as so many streams to refresh thy soul. Of assertory Scriptures, see John 6:39; 10:28; I John 2:19. Of promissory Scriptures, see Isaiah 54:10; Jer. 33:15, 20-21; I Cor. 1:8. Of comparative Scriptures, see Psalm. 1:3; 125; I John 4:14. The principal scope of all which is to show the indefectible nature of true grace in the saints.

And now, how this should refresh thy drooping soul and make thee gird up the loins of thy mind since thou dost "not run as one uncertain neither fightest as one that beats the air" (I Cor. 9:26) but art so secured from total apostasy as thou seest thou art by all these things, O bless ye the Lord.

Objection 2: But the Lord seems to be departed from my soul. God is afar off from me and troubles are near. I seem to be in such a case as Saul was when the Philistines made war upon him and God was departed from him—therefore, I shall fall.

Solution 2: Not so, for there are two sorts of divine desertions; the one is absolute when the Lord utterly forsakes his creatures so that they shall never behold his face more. The other is limited and respective, as he forsook his own Son and often does his own elect. Of this kind, some desertions are only cautious to prevent sin; some are merely probational to try grace; and others castigatory, to chastise our negligence and carelessness. Now, though I have not a word of comfort to speak in the case of total and absolute desertions, yet of the latter (which doubtless is thy case) much may be said by way of support, be it whichever the three sorts it will, or in, what degree it will.

1. For this hath been the case of many precious souls (Psalm 22:1-2; 77:2; 88:9; Job 13:24-26). This was poor Mr. Glover's case, as you will find in his story, and it continued till he came within sight of the stake; therefore, no new or strange thing hath happened unto you.

2. The Lord by this will advantage thee for perseverance, not only as they are cautioned against sin, but as they make thee hold Christ the faster and prize his presence at an higher rate when he shall be pleased to graciously manifest himself to thee again (Song of Solomon 3:4).

3. This shall not abide forever—it is but a little cloud and will blow over. It is but for a moment, and that moment's darkness ushers in everlasting light (Isa. 54:7). Lastly, the light of God's countenance shall not only be restored certainly, but it shall be restored seasonably—when the darkness is greatest, thy troubles at the highest, and thy hopes largest. He is a God of judgment and knows how to time his own mercies (Psalm 138:3).

Objection 3: But I am a weak woman or a young person—how shall I be able to confess Christ before rulers and look great ones in the face?

Solution 3: Christ delights to make his power known in such (II Cor. 12:9), for he affects not social glory.

1. "Thou shalt be held up, for God is able to make thee stand" (Rom. 14:4). Thou that art sensible of thine own infirmity mayest run to that promise.

2. Such poor weak creatures shall endure and be stronger, but if they are self-confident, they will fall. "Even the youths shall faint, and be weary, and the young men utterly fall. But they that wait upon the Lord shall renew their strength. They shall mount up with wings as eagles, run and not be weary, walk and not faint" (Isaiah 40:30-31). Youth are bold, daring, and confident persons that trust to their own strength, to whom such as wait upon the Lord stand here opposed. They shall faint, but these shall renew their strength. Art thou one that waitest and dependest upon an all-sufficient God in the sense of thine own weakness? This promise then is for thee.

3. You may furnish yourselves at pleasure with examples of the mighty power of God resting upon such as you are out of our own martyrology.

Thomas Drowry, the poor blind boy, Fox's Book of Martyrs, vol. 3. p. 703. What a presence of spirit was with him when examined by the Chancellor!

Eulalia, a virgin of about 12 years of age—see how she acted above those years, yea, above the power of nature. Fox's Book of Martyrs, vol. 1. p. 120. Tender women, yea, children, act above themselves when assisted by a strong God.

And thus you have some help offered to you by a weak hand in your present and most important work. The Lord carry home all with power upon your hearts that if God call you to suffer for him, you may say as Paul did, "I am now ready to be offered up, and the time of my departure is at hand. I have fought a good fight, I have finished my course, I have kept the faith; henceforth there is laid up for me a crown of righteousness which God the righteous Judge shall give me at that day; and not to me only, but to them also which love his appearing" (II Tim. 4:6-8). And as you expect so to finish your course with joy, be diligent in the use of all means to prepare and make yourselves ready to follow the call of God, whether it be to bonds, or to death, for the name of the Lord Jesus.

APPENDIX:
OUTLINE OF THE BOOK

1. **Theme of the Book: Prepare to Suffer (Acts 21:13)**
2. **Why God calls His people to Suffer**
    I. To illustrate His glory
        A. To clear up His righteous name by disciplining their sin. He hates sin not a jot the less because it is found in His own people (Amos 3:2).
        B. To give a fit opportunity to manifest the glory of His power in their support and of His wisdom in the marvelous ways of their escape and deliverance.
    II. To promote His people's happiness
        A. By mortifying corruptions in their hearts
        B. To prove to themselves the sincerity of their faith and thus remove their doubts
        C. To free the church of hypocrites
        D. To endear believers to one another (Gal. 6:1)
        E. To awaken them to their duties and teach them to pray more frequently, spiritually, and fervently

3. **Forewarnings of Suffering**
    I. Circumstances that precede or provoke suffering
        A. Adulterating of God's worship
        B. Obstinacy under gentler strokes and lesser judgments
        C. Spiritual dullness and apathy
        D. The persecution of God's ministers and people
        E. The premature death of godly and useful men
        F. Decay of the life a godliness among God's people that remain
        G. Animosities and divisions among God's people
    II. Why God forewarns His people of suffering
        A. To prevent the execution by repentance
        B. To make the execution more tolerable
        C. To leave the incorrigible inexcusable

4. The Necessity of a Prepared Heart for Suffering

I. Preparation for suffering proves the sincerity of our faith

II. Preparation for suffering prevents our own offense at carrying our cross

III. It convinces and awakens a drowsy world

IV. The Spirit of God sets an honorable character to it

V. It influences a Christian's stability in the evil day

VI. It is a very high testimony of our love to Jesus Christ when we show our willingness to take our lot with Him and follow Him wherever he goes

VII. It proves that our will is subdued to God

VIII. God often excuses them from suffering whose heart is prepared to suffer

IX. Those who have prepared their hearts to suffer but who fall are more likely to rise back up

5. The Necessity of a Saving Work of Grace for Suffering

I. There must be true conversion

    A. Self must be dethroned in the heart

    B. Christ and His interests must be supreme

II. The spirit must be raised above the dangers and difficulties of this world

    A. By having a high view of eternal things which shrinks all temporal things

    B. By valuing and measuring all things in light of eternity

    C. By the Spirit of Christ infusing grace

III. The will must be subject to the will of God

IV. The heart must be composed, fixed, and determined to follow the Lord through all hazards and difficulties.

V. The soul must have a continual supply of strength and refreshment

    A. Not from fallible things but

    B. From God's Word and prayer

VI. There must be a real work of grace within the soul

    A. The Christian must suffer for true Christian principles

    B. The Christian must suffer in a Christian manner

    C. The Christian must suffer by the grace of God

6. The Nature of a Saving Work of Grace

I. There must be a true change

    A. Not a change of the judgment of error to truth

    B. Not a change of man's practice or manners

    C. Not a change from mere morality to mere formality in religion

    D. Nor is it a change of status, such as justification makes

    E. Not a change of the essence of man

II. What the change is—it is the infusion of new habits of grace into the old faculties which immediately depose sin from its dominion over the soul and deliver up the soul into the hands and government of Christ so that it lives no more to itself but to Christ. It is a:

    A. New creation (Gal 6:15)

    B. New man (Ephesians 4:24)

    C. New birth (John 3:3)

    D. Christ formed in us (Gal. 4:19)

    E. Change of judgment, will, affections and practice

    F. The almighty power of God working within and throughout

    G. The Spirit overpowering the understanding with clear demonstrations and silencing all objections, pleas, and pretences to the contrary

    H. Willingness to sacrifice estate, liberty, name and life

    I. Uniform in all of those in whom it is wrought

III. The change encompasses the whole man—body, soul, and practice

    A. Views temporal things as dung, dross, and vanity

    B. Esteems Jesus Christ as the wisdom and power of God

    C. Loves the saints

    D. Strictness and duty are the only things desirable

    E. The will is totally submitted to God

    F. Weaned from earthly enjoyments

    G. Desires Jesus Christ above all things

    H. When alone thoughts are of Christ and delight in Him

    I. Chief aim is to be pleasing to God

IV. The change prepares a man for glorious and singular service to God

    A. If God calls a man to a duty, there is a principle within closing with the command without and moving the soul freely and spontaneously to duty

159

B. Grace will enable the soul to break its way to God through all the interposing obstacles and discouragements.

7. Evidences of a Saving Work of Grace
I. What is the evidence of a work of saving grace
A. The Spirit's shining upon his own work in the hearts of believers, thereby enabling them sensibly to see and feel it to their own satisfaction
1. It is attainable to a very high degree
2. Some believers have mourned for the want of it (David, Job, etc.)
3. During its continuance, it is the sweetest thing in the world
4. The Spirit acts arbitrarily in its continuance and removal
5. Few live in a constant and quiet fruition of it
6. God has given a sure light and sufficient means in the diligent use of its improvement
a. Scripture-light
b. Light of experience
c. The light of the Spirit
II. The advantage of a saving work of grace for suffering
A. This grace of love enables him victoriously to break through all difficulties and discouragements
B. It takes out the sinking weight of affliction
C. It is a fountain of joy and comfort in the darkest and saddest hour
III. Rules for attaining evidence of a saving work of grace
A. Make it your business to improve your graces
B. Be sure to try your faith by the proper marks
C. Take heed of sins that violate the conscience
D. Labor to avoid those common mistakes Christians make in judging their state
1. Do not question the truth of your grace when you fall short of God's law if you failings are against the bent and resolution of your heart
2. Do not question the truth of your grace because it was not wrought in the same manner as in others

3. Do not question the truth of your grace because you do not experience ravishing joys and transports of love

4. Do not question the truth of your grace because of the attainments of some hypocrites who in some things may excel thee

    a. Self is never dethroned in the hypocrite

    b. The hypocrite does not hate every sin

    c. The hypocrite is motivated by external advantages rather than by the bent and inclination of the heart towards God

5. Do not question the truth of your grace because you grow not as sensibly as other Christians

    a. Do not measure yourselves by your desires, for the Christian aims high and grasps all

    b. Do not compare yourselves with those who have larger capacities, time, and advantages than you

    c. Do not compare your graces with other men's gifts which you mistake for graces

    d. Do not think that all growth is upward in joy, peace, and comfort whereas you may grow deep in mortification and humiliation

8. The Necessity of Improving Faith

  I. Faith makes a weak soul strong and able to bear

    A. It removes fear

    B. It turns the soul to Christ

  II. It lightens a Christians burdens by

    A. Committing the matter to Christ and leaving it with Him

    B. Discovering present good in our troubles

    C. Foreseeing the end and removal of our troubles (II Cor. 4:17)

    D. Comparing our suffering with others who are suffering more

    E. Advancing God's glory and filling up that what is lacking in Christ's sufferings (Col. 1:27)

    F. Enjoying the special manifest presence of Christ in suffering for Him

  III. How to improve Faith

    A. Attend diligently to the teaching and preaching of the Word

    B. Improve your use of the Lord's Day by faith

C. Rouse up dull habits and act upon your faith

D. Beg of the Lord to increase your faith

E. Improve times of affliction for the building up of your faith

F. Keep catalogues of all your remarkable experiences, and treasure them up as food to your faith for times to come

G. Beware of sense, which is the supplanter of faith

9. The Necessity of Christian Fortitude

I. You must rouse up and awaken your courage for God

A. Because the success and prevalence of Satan's temptations in the hour of persecution depends upon the fainting and overthrow of this grace

B. Because this is the grace that honors Jesus Christ abundantly when you are brought upon the stage for Him

C. Because your own peace is wrapped up in it as well as God's glory

D. Because your magnanimity is of special use to other saints who are following you in the same path of sufferings

II. What is Christian fortitude

A. Holy boldness not a natural or sinful boldness

B. It is expressed about duties for truth not error

C. It is for the interest of Christ not of the flesh

D. It perseveres when duties (i.e., meeting with the saints, prayer, preaching of the Word, etc.) are surrounded and beset with difficulties and dangers

E. The fountain whence it flows is faith and that as it respects the command and call of God to duty

F. Rules for promoting and improving it

1. Get a weaned heart from all earthly enjoyments

2. Suffer not guilt to lie upon your conscience

3. Know God's call, especially in difficult services

4. Get right notions and apprehensions of your enemies

a. They are poor, weak enemies

b. The little power they have is limited by your God who hath the bounding and ordering of it

c. They carry guilt upon them which makes them more timorous than you

162

      d. They only use carnal weapons against you which cannot touch your souls

      e. Your enemies are God's enemies, and God hath espoused your cause and quarrel

5. Labor to engage the presence of God with you in all places and conditions

6. Get a high estimation of Jesus Christ and all His concernments

7. Beware you be not cheated with maxims of carnal policy that are mistaken for Christian prudence

8. Look upon the inside of troubles for Christ as well as upon the outside of them

9. View the issue and reward of suffering by an eye of faith

10. Propound to yourselves the best patterns and examples

10. The Necessity of a Mortified Heart to all Earthly and Temporal Enjoyments

I. Unless your heart be mortified to these things, it will be very hard to part with them in a suffering hour

II. Mortification of corruptions is that which recovers a healthful state of soul

III. Your corruptions must be mortified lest during a suffering time of temptation they sweep away all your convictions and resolutions

IV. Unless you be diligent and successful in this work, though you suffer, yet it will not be like a Christian, your religion will be disgraced for which you suffer

V. Many longings and hankerings after earthly enjoyments and comforts will prove a snare to you

VI. The necessity to mortify four special corruptions

    A. Mortify love of the world and earthly possessions

      1. It's idolatry and unfaithfulness to Christ

      2. The more you prize it the more you will be tormented by it

      3. It is an empty glory that is passing away

      4. Set your heart on Christ and the things above

      5. By your love and delight in worldly things you furnish the devil with the chief bait he hath to catch and destroy your souls.

      6. Live in light of eternity

B. Mortify your ambition and vain affectation of the repute and credit of the world

    1. The holiest of men have been despised by the world

    2. Christ may be scoffed at because of your behavior—therefore, be willing to be scoffed at for Him

    3. It is much better to be reproached by men for discharging duty than by your own consciences for the neglect of it

    4. Always remember that you neither stand nor fall at the world's judgment

    5. There is a worth and excellency in the reproaches of Christ

    6. Should reproaches for Christ scare you, then though you should escape the reproaches of men, you shall fall under the everlasting contempt of God

C. Mortify your inordinate affections of liberty, pleasure, and delicate living

    1. There is no place but may be delectable to you if your heart be heavenly and the presence of God be engaged with you

    2. No prison keeper can keep the Comforter from you if you be the Lord's prisoners

    3. If God exchanged for you a hell for a prison, have you any cause to complain?

    4. However cruel men are, the Lord Jesus is kind and tender-hearted to his prisoners

    5. A prison hath been perfumed by the best and holiest of men

    6. Should you, to avoid a prison, commit a sin instead of being man's prisoner, you shall be locked up by God, for he hath a prison for your souls even in this world

    7. Consider what a ground of comfort God hath laid in that word to obviate the fears and terrors incident to us in such a condition

    8. You do not know what a mercy may be in it

D. Get a heart mortified to the excessive and inordinate love of life

    1. Though life be very dear, yet Jesus Christ is ten thousand times dearer than thy life

2. If by shrinking from Christ you should protract a miserable life for a few days longer, in the mean time you have lost that which is better than life

3. If you have cordially covenanted with Christ (as all sincere believers have done) then you have yielded up your lives to Him, to be disposed of for His glory

4. To die for Christ is one of the highest testimonies of your love to Christ that you are capable of

5. Why should you decline even a violent death for Christ when the bitterness of death shall so soon be past

6. Think what a death Christ suffered for you in which the fullness of the wrath of God and man met together so that He was sore amazed; yet "with desire did He desire" it for your sake

7. Think what a life you shall have with Christ as soon as you are delivered up to and for Him

11. The Methods and Mysteries of Satan's Temptations

I. He that is well acquainted with the methods of temptation will be better able to descry the first approaches and beginnings of it, which is to more than half conquer it

II. He that is well acquainted with Satan's methods of tempting will not only discern it sooner than another but also knows his work and duty and how to manage the conflict with it

III. He that is best acquainted with the mystery of temptation he can maintain his ground against it and shall be the persevering Christian under persecutions

IV. Wherein the force and efficacy of temptation lies

    A. The power of temptation lies in the kind and nature of the temptation

        1. Unusual temptations as the people of God are but rarely troubled with

        2. Mark them for most dangerous temptations that are adapted and suited to your proper sin or evil constitution

        3. When it is a spiritual temptation which rises undiscernibly out of the Christian's duties

    B. The strength and efficacy of temptation lies much in the skill and policy of Satan in the management of it

1. Satan works by employing such instruments to manage his temptations as are least suspected and have the greatest influence

2. Satan works by the orderly disposition and ranging of his temptations, beginning with little things first, and then by degrees working over to greater

3. Satan works by endeavoring to engage the soul upon his own ground. I mean to tempt him from his station and duty where God sets and expects to find him

4. Satan works by not presenting the temptation till the soul be prepared to receive it

5. Satan works by tiring our souls with a long continuance of temptations

6. Satan works by falling most violently upon them when they are lowest and most prostrate in their spirits and comforts

C. Temptation lies in that secret correspondence Satan holds with our bosom enemy—our flesh

   1. Rules for the escaping or conquering of those temptations that are incidental to a suffering state

      a. Labor to cut off the temptations of inordinate love of life, estate, liberty and ease

         i. Mortify self-love and creature-love

         ii. Let your heart be loosened and weaned from them, and then the temptation hath lost its strength

      b. Secure to yourselves an interest in the heavenly glory

      c. Settle this principle in your heart as that which you will never depart from—that it is better for you to fall into any suffering than into the least sin

      d. Believe that God hath cursed and blasted all the ways of sin so that they shall never be a shelter to any soul that flies to them for refuge

      e. Live up to this principle that there is no policy like sincerity and godly simplicity

      f. Consider sadly what the consequence of yielding up yourselves to temptations will be

         i. The name of God will be dreadfully reproached

ii. A fatal stumbling-block is laid before the blind world

iii. The hearts of many upright ones will be made sad

iv. A dreadful wound it will be to thine own conscience

v. One hour's sleep of security may keep you many days and nights waking upon the rack of horror

g. Never engage a temptation in your own strength but go forth against it trembling in yourselves and relying on divine aids and assistances

h. Let the days of your temptation be days of strong cries and supplications

i. Dwell upon the consideration of those choice encouragements that God hath laid up in the world for such a time

  i. Though God give Satan leave to tempt you, yet you are still in His hand to preserve you

  ii. That whilst Satan is sifting and trying you on earth, Christ is interceding for you in heaven

j. Be content till God open a door out of your temptations

12. The Necessity of Prayer

I. That prayer is the outlet of troubles and the best way the poor Christian hath to ease his heart when surcharged with sorrow

A. This opens and gives a vent to troubles

B. It gives our troubles a diversion and so a cure

C. By praying over them they are not only diverted but sanctified, and so cease to be distracting or destroying troubles

II. As prayer gives a vent to our troubles, so it gives an inlet to unspeakable comforts and consolations

III. Prayer begets and maintains holy courage and magnanimity in evil times

IV. Prayer is a duty you may perform at any time or in any condition

V. You must strive to excel in prayer, forasmuch as no grace within, or service without, can thrive without it

VI. Depend on the Spirit's assistance for prayer

A. He excites the heart to the duty

B. He suggests the matter of our prayers

C. He stirs up suitable affections in prayer
VII. How to improve prayer
    A. Be more frequent in duty
    B. Take heed not to grieve the Holy Spirit
    C. Depend on the Spirit
    D. Give glory to Him when He helps you
    E. Search your hearts
    F. Labor for impressions more and pumping out expressions less

13 The Necessity of Depending on Christ

I. Consider the Christian's own insufficiency even in the strength and height of all his acquirements and preparations

II. Consider that it is the great design of God in the gospel to exalt His Son and to have all glory attributed and ascribed to Him

III. A Christian is constantly to depend upon Christ notwithstanding all His own preparations and inherent qualifications, because the activity even of inherent grace depends upon him

IV. In living a life of dependence upon Christ your security lies

V. What dependence upon Christ is
    A. It is not to deny grace wrought in us by the Spirit
    B. It is not an excuse for neglect of spiritual duties
    C. It is seeing and acknowledging the infinite sufficiency and fullness that is in Christ
    D. It is seeing the necessary dependence that all our graces have upon Him
    E. It lies in looking off from your own grace whenever you are put upon the acting of it and looking by an eye of faith for acceptation to Christ

VI. Several considerations regarding dependence on Christ
    A. You have little reason to rely upon the strength of your own graces for you may be easily deceived in that matter and think you have much more grace than you have
    B. Suppose you have much grace—however, do you not have strong corruptions, and may you not meet with strong temptations also
    C. Whatever measures of grace you have arrived at, yet all is not able to secure you from falling if God withhold or withdraw His aids and influences

D. Nothing more provokes the Lord to withdraw His Spirit and let you fall than this sin of self-confidence

E. If God permit you to fall, (as doubtless He will, if you be self-conceited) then the more eminent you have been or are for grace, the more will the name of God be reproached by your fall

F. Have you not sad experience of your own weakness from day to day in your lesser trials? Consult your former experiences, and they will tell you what weaklings you are

G. Hath Christ given you more grace than others? Then how much more hath He obliged you to honor Him thereby?

14. The Church's Lack of Preparation for Suffering

I. The politic and hypocritical professors whose hearts were never set right at first cannot be steadfast when trials come

II. There are others that may be truly godly and have the root of the matter in them who are yet far from an actual readiness

A. Upon how many of the saints is the spirit of slumber poured out?

B. How many are seized by a private and worldly spirit?

C. How many poor Christians are of a low and timorous spirit, ready to tremble at the shaking of a leaf?

D. How many poor Christians among us are to this day dark and cloudy in their evidences for heaven?

15. The Necessity of Preparing for Greater Trials

I. Consider the many calls which God hath given you to this work of preparing for suffering

A. By the Word

B. By the rod

C. By prodigious and portentous signs in the heavens and earth

II. Suffering proves fatal and destructive to some but only to those who are secure and careless

III. Preparation for suffering will best answer the grace of God in affording you such choice helps and advantages as you have enjoyed

IV. Remember how ready the Lord Jesus was to suffer the hardest and vilest things for you, such as

A. Suffering the dignity of His person—the Son of God, the darling of the Father, becoming a man

169

B. That He suffered in the prime and flower of His years when full of life and sense and more capable of exquisite sense of pain than others

C. The manner of His death—the cross

D. All this while God hid His face from Him and poured out His wrath upon Him in our stead

16. Words of Comfort to Trembling Souls

I. Objection 1: I will fail in a suffering hour because of the deceitfulness of the heart

Answer 1: Though the heart is such, you shall not totally fall because

A. God's eternal electing love

B. The covenant of grace

1. The Author of this covenant is not a fickle creature but a faithful God

2. God hath established the covenant with you in the blood of Christ

3. Remember and draw comfort from that strict and intimate union that is between Christ and thee

a. Whatever He is, or hath, it is for thee

b. This union with His person secures thy feeble graces from perishing

c. It implies thy perseverance because by this union thou becomest an integral part of Christ's body which would be mutilated and defective should thou be cut off and lost

d. Thou shalt not be lost because of the prevalent intercession of Jesus Christ in the heavens for all His saints in all their trials here on earth

C. Your salvation is secure because of the Spirit of Christ which dwells and abides in thee and hath begun His saving work upon thee

1. His honor is pledged and engaged to perfect it

2. The grace He hath already wrought in thee may give thee yet further and fuller assurance of its preservation, inasmuch as it hath the nature of a seal, pledge, and earnest of the whole

170

3. Your salvation is secure based on those multitudes of assertory, promissory, and comparative scriptures

II. Objection 2: The Lord has departed from me

Answer 2: Not so, for there are two sorts of Divine desertions; the one is absolute, when the Lord utterly forsakes His creatures; the other is limited and respective, as He forsook His own Son and often does His own elect.

A. Many precious believers have experienced temporary desertions

B. The Lord by this will advantage thee for perseverance, not only as they are cautioned against sin, but as they make thee hold Christ the faster and prize His presence at an higher rate

C. This shall not abide for ever—it is but a little cloud and will blow over

III. Objection 3: But I am a weak woman or a young person—how shall I be able to confess Christ before rulers and look great ones in the face?

Answer 3: Christ delights to make His power known in such for He affects not social glory

A. Thou shalt be held up, for God is able to make thee stand

B. Such poor weak creatures shall endure and be stronger, but if they are self-confident, they will fall

C. You may furnish yourselves at pleasure with examples of the mighty power of God resting upon such as you are out of our own martyrology

Made in the USA
San Bernardino,
CA